CARDINALS HANDBOOK ™

Stories, Stats and Stuff About Louisville™ Basketball

By Russ Brown
Foreword by Denny Crum

Printed in the United States of America by
Mennonite Press, Inc.

ISBN 1-880652-75-7

PHOTO CREDITS All photographs were supplied
by the University of Louisville.

ACKNOWLEDGMENTS

ACKNOWLEDGMENTS

For Mary Jo
—R.B.

I'm indebted to several people for their help with this book.

Foremost, I don't think I would have undertaken this project without the promise of help from Mike Smith, a former newspaper sportswriter who now works in the University of Louisville news and public information department. Mike has written his own book on U of L basketball, *Top of the Cards*, and he allowed me access to his exhaustive research along with helping report other aspects of the book. Without his unselfish contributions of his time and effort, my job would have been 10 times as hard.

Another great source of information was Gary Tuell, a former sports information director at U of L, who did a remarkably thorough job in compiling a historical account of U of L basketball in *Above The Rim*, published in 1988.

Then there's Kenny Klein and his fine sports information staff at U of L. Kenny provided the statistics and records, plus much of the biographical material on former players, and recommended me to editor Bruce Janssen to be the author of this book. Kenny, U of L Athletic Director Bill Olsen, and Associate AD Mike Pollio were instrumental in providing clips, photos and other research material.

I'm also grateful to coach Denny Crum, former assistant coaches Jerry Jones and Wade Houston, and numerous ex-players for their cooperation and assistance.

Dale Moss, a news columnist for *The Courier-Journal* and a long-time friend, persuaded me to take on this project when I was wavering because of the time commitment. And I'm indebted to copy editor Dave Roos, also of *The Courier-Journal,* for helping wrestle the manuscript into its final form with a minimum of bloodshed.

Finally, I'd like to thank my lovely wife, Mary Jo, for her encouragement, support and patience, not only while I was writing this book but during 30-plus years of marriage.

—Russ Brown

DEDICATION

Derek Smith, who died at age 34 on August 9, 1996, while on a cruise with his family, was one of the most popular players in University of Louisville basketball history. And not just because he was a key member of the Cardinals' 1980 national championship team.

This book is dedicated to the memory of Derek Smith

First, Smith endeared himself to U of L fans with his relentless intensity and hustle on the basketball court. Then, after his career had ended, he continued to win friends with his bright personality and his eagerness to give both his time and money to help worthwhile causes in the Louisville area, particularly those involving kids.

Smith, who came to U of L as a 16-year-old freshman from little Hogansville, Ga., with all his personal belongings in a grocery sack, had a ready smile and an infectious enthusiasm that made him instantly likeable to everyone he met.

"You couldn't help but love Derek," U of L coach Denny Crum said. "He was such a fine gentleman and a giving person. He was just a wonderful, wonderful guy."

"Derek was self-motivated to be the best at everything he did, and that attitude had a positive influence on everyone he met," said U of L Athletic Director Bill Olsen, who recruited Smith. "Derek did things right. He never asked for anything, he always gave. His death was a tremendous loss to society."

Smith was the second-leading scorer on U of L's '80 championship team, averaging 14.8 points per game along with a team-high 8.3 rebounds. He was also a catalyst for two more clubs, the 1981 squad that was knocked out of the NCAA Tournament by Arkansas on U.S. Reed's half-court shot, and the '82 team that lost to Georgetown 50-46 in the Final Four semifinals. He still ranks as U of L's No. 4 all-time scorer with 1,826 points.

Smith knew the value of a college eduation. So, following a nine-year career in the National Basketball Association, he returned to U of L and graduated with a degree in communications in 1992. For the graduation ceremony, he wore his basketball uniform — No.43 — under his gown, then threw a party and invited many of the professors who had helped him attain his goal.

For Louisville fans, there will never be another No. 43.

— *Russ Brown*

FOREWORD

In the past several years, NCAA basketball has truly become a national treasure, capturing the attention of every corner of the nation. But nowhere has the glamour and added exposure been felt more than in Kentucky and Indiana, where fans put basketball right up there with breathing and eating as far as importance is concerned.

When I came to Louisville in 1971, I had no idea that I would be staying here for more than a quarter of a century. Yet one very major reason I took the job in the first place was that here was a university that was already well established as one of the premier basketball programs in the nation. What has happened since has been an incredible experience for me.

In my time I have read many college basketball books, including several written solely about the University of Louisville, and I can truly say that this one is one of the finest. I have known Russ Brown for many years now and and he has my highest respect. I find him to be a thorough, fair, and an overall excellent sportswriter. His book offers not only a concise and condensed history of U of L basketball since its inception in 1911, but it is the first book to highlight our accomplishments of the 1990s.

Since winning our latest championship in 1986, I feel Louisville has maintained its fine tradition, as you will read in this book. I think you will find it a must for both the average follower of the game to the very serious Cardinal fan. It is loaded with interesting stories, sidelight features, historical statistics, more than 100 photographs, and even a number of trivia questions.

Here, you will read about all the stars the university has produced and you will read about people whose accomplishments have long since been forgotten. You will also read about the great rivalries with Western in the 1940s, Dayton in the 1950s and more recently, with teams such as Memphis and, of course, Kentucky. Above all, you will find it well written, entertaining, and educational.

I hope you enjoy Russ Brown's book as much as I have.

— *Denny Crum, U of L basketball coach*

TABLE OF CONTENTS

The Louisville Tradition

Basketball is special to Kentuckians. The sport permeates everyday life from offices to farms, from coal mines to neighborhood drug stores. It is more than just a sport played in the cold winter months. It is a source of pride and a year-round cause for anticipation, hope, and celebration. The University of Louisville program has supplied its fans with all of that for decades.

Legendary coach Bernard "Peck" Hickman, a Basketball Hall of Fame nominee, arrived on the U of L campus in 1944 to begin a remarkable string of 46 consecutive winning seasons. For 23 seasons, Hickman laid an impressive foundation for the Cardinal program. John Dromo, an assistant coach under Hickman for 19 years, continued the program in outstanding fashion following Hickman's retirement. And since 1971, Denny Crum has guided the Cardinals to even higher acclaim.

The school's successes include national championships in the NCAA (1980 and 1986), NIT (1956) and the NAIB (1948). Louisville is the only school in the nation to have claimed the championship in all three major tournaments. The Cardinals have appeared in the NCAA tournament 25 times, fourth all-time behind Kentucky (37), UCLA (30), and North Carolina (30). Crum has directed the Cardinals to 19 of those appearances.

Louisville has played in the Final Four seven times, including four times in the 1980s. Only six schools — UCLA (14), North Carolina (12), Duke (10), Kansas (10), Kentucky (10) and Ohio State (8) — have reached

While schools such as UCLA, Indiana, Kentucky and North Carolina referred to their programs as dynasties, Louisville cheerleaders make reference to the Cardinal Empire!

the Final Four more often. Indiana matches the Cards' seven Final Fours.

Crum alone has taken six teams to the Final Four. Only John Wooden (12), Dean Smith (9) and Mike Krzyzewski (7) have taken more.

THE EARLY YEARS

In the beginning there was women's basketball at the University of Louisville. The women, coached by William Gardiner, began a winning tradition before there even was a men's team. But in 1911 Gardiner agreed to also take on coaching duties of a men's team that played only a three-game schedule. The first opponent was the Louisville YMCA team. The game was played on January 27, 1912, at the Tharp School Gymnasium at Fifth and Zane streets.

The YMCA won 35-3 in a game in which, according to *The Courier-Journal*, the U of L team "was totally outclassed." The first-year schedule concluded with a pair of demolishings at the hands of Moore's Hill, a small college in Indiana, 28-13 and 51-7.

FIRST CONFERENCE The future of men's basketball took a turn for the better when on February 5, 1912, the team was invited to join the Southern Intercollegiate Athletic Association. Other members included Kentucky, North Carolina, Vanderbilt and Virginia.

Gardiner, however, decided to step down as coach and by doing so became the sole U of L mentor not to win a single game. Although the 1912-13 team had no coach, it registered a 2-3 record. The first victory came in the second game, a 24-20 win over the New Albany YMCA. The other triumph was in the last game of the season, on February 28, with the victim being Moore's Hill.

Losses were dealt by the Louisville YMCA (25-18), Kentucky (34-10 in Lexington) and Tennessee (24-16).

In all, between that first game with the Louisville YMCA in 1912 and the beginning of the Peck Hickman era in 1944, U of L won 187 games and lost 235. It had 10 winning seasons, 16 losing ones and twice played .500 ball.

In the early years at U of L, women's basketball was more popular than men's. However, between 1911 and about 1915 only females were allowed to watch the women play. The only men allowed in the gym for the women's games were the officials.

CAPTAIN ETHELMAE TUELL

BUSINESS MGR. ADA SARA LINKER

CHAMPIONSHIP CUP

On three occasions, in 1916-17, 1922-23 and again in 1942-43, Louisville was unable to field a team. In 1916-17 and 1922-23 the finances simply weren't available, and in 1942-43 World War II caused the cancellation of many sporting events.

Horace Carter was captain of the 1921-22 team that won only once in 14 games.

LACK OF FUNDS During the 33 years that preceded the Hickman era, no coach served more than five years. After Gardiner left following that initial season, there was no head coach until Earl Ford and Jim Parks shared the duty in the 1918-19 season, winning seven of 11 games. They were followed by three coaches who each remained only one season, Tuley Brucker (6-5 in 1919-20), Jimmie Powers (3-8 in 1920-21), and Dr. J. T. O'Rourke (1-13 in 1921-22). The 1921-22 season is remembered primarily because this was the last U of L regular-season schedule that included Kentucky until 1983-84.

The Wildcats won both of those 1922 games, 38-14 in Louisville and 29-22 in Lexington. It was another eight years before Adolph Rupp arrived in Lexington.

After a one-year layoff in 1922-23, Fred Enke became the U of L coach. Enke's first team won only four of 17 games but, as reported in *Above the Rim*, it was one that had historical significance, centering around a 40-19 loss to Georgetown College on January 4, 1924. It was at this game that a U of L pep band performed for the first time and, secondly, a young *Courier-Journal* sportswriter covered the Cardinals for the first time. His name was Earl Ruby, and he would remain at the C-J for 63 years.

In 1924-25, Enke became the first to coach a U of L team for more than one season, with his club going 10-7. But at the end of the year, he resigned to take a similar position at Arizona, where he would remain until 1961.

KING STAYS FIVE YEARS Enke was succeeded in 1925-26 by Tom King, who remained for five seasons, winning 44 and losing 31. Edward Weber stayed two years, winning 20 and losing 18. Weber's 1931-32 team went 15-7, the most victories in a single season for any U of L team to that point. At the end of the season, Weber resigned to take a position with Kentucky Military Institute in Lyndon.

THE MONEY YEARS Weber's successor was C.V. (Red) Money, who came to U of L from Hanover College. He would remain four years, winning 46 and losing 40. During Money's first three years, only four games were against non-Kentucky teams. In his final season, 1935-36, Louisville was 14-11 and faced eight opponents who were from outside the commonwealth. Most notable was Indiana, which crushed the Cards 48-26.

Following Money's departure, Louisville entered the darkest period of its basketball existence. During the next seven seasons (spanning eight years) the Cardinals won only 29 games while losing 86. Their coaches were Lawrence E. Apitz for four years, John Heldman for two years and, in 1943-44, the coaching duties were shared by C. Spec. Harold Church and C. Spec. Walter Casey, both Navy personnel.

IT'S DOWNHILL Apitz (10-52) had the least success. In two seasons, the Cardinals defeated only Berea, twice. As *Courier-Journal* reporter Larry Boeck said, "in Louisville's case instead of 'God Bless America' it should be 'God Bless Berea.' "

"Jolly John" Heldman, the athletic director, not only inherited a program on the decline but was also faced with the dilemma of having no scholarships to offer. Most opponents in 1940-41 were at least offering players partial scholarships. After losing its first 11 games, Louisville finally presented Heldman with his first victory by beating Berea 44-36 on February 12, 1941. The only other win came in the final game of the regular season, over Transylvania.

WORLD WAR II The following year marked the first time in six seasons that the Cardinals won more than four games in a single season by going 7-10. This would be Louisville's last losing season until 1990-91.

The havoc of World War II caused the cancellation of many college basketball seasons, including Louisville's in 1942-43. But the next year, basketball at Louisville resumed with a new look because most of the players were Navy veterans. Therefore, for the next two years U of L was known as the Sea Cards. In one game that year, a 53-51 overtime loss to a team from Bowman Field in Louisville, civilian spectators were barred from attending. U of L finished 10-10.

CARDINALS QUIZ

1. Peck Hickman (U of L) and Adolph Rupp (Kentucky) recorded their initial wins against the same opponent — Hickman in 1944 and Rupp in 1930. What was the school they defeated?

Back From The Brink

Coach Bernard (Peck) Hickman

When Bernard (Peck) Hickman assumed the role of head coach in August 1944, the program was on the verge of extinction. In the previous 10 seasons, U of L had played 154 games and lost 106 of them. It had not enjoyed a winning season since going 14-11 in 1935-36.

Hickman grew up in Muhlenberg County and played at Western Kentucky University under the legendary Ed Diddle, who inspired him to go into coaching himself.

In 1944, Louisville Athletic Director John Heldman offered him his chance. Hickman's dilemma, though, was that he had a good-paying high school job at Valley on the outskirts of Louisville. U of L was unable to match his salary of $3,600 a year.

"Peck, you come highly recommended," Heldman said. "In fact, Mr. Diddle says you're about the smartest player he ever coached. We think you might be able to save our program at U of L." Nobody he was associated with, including his wife, encouraged Hickman to make the move. But after weighing his options, he notified Heldman that he would take the job. "My goal is to be a college coach and I may not get another chance," he said. On August 9, 1944, *The Louisville Times* announced Hickman's hiring.

THE 1944-45 SEASON Hickman inherited the task of bringing respectability to a basketball program that had none. And he was to do it predominantly with players assigned from the military and on a budget of a meager $3,000.

Even though Belknap Gym seated comfortably only about 600, a typical crowd would fill about half the place. The uniforms were old and worn, but with his tight budget he could hardly replace them with new ones. With the war on, there were travel restrictions and a lack of transportation. Therefore, the 19-game schedule included only one game outside Kentucky or Indiana. That was against Marshall in neighboring Huntington, W.Va. Also, he had no assistant coach and no trainer, although Lt. Douglas Taylor, a faculty member, assisted on a voluntary basis.

To solve the uniform problem, Heldman's wife went to a second-hand dry goods store on Main Street, purchased some material and made them herself.

Although Hickman was only slightly older than most of his players, it soon became apparent that he was skillful and highly organized. "Coach made the best use of what practice time he had," said George Hauptfuhrer, who like

CARDINALS QUIZ

2. Louisville's first basketball All-American was who?

most of the players was in the Navy's V-12 program. "He kept us in wonderful condition and taught us from the beginning to make intelligent, on-the-spot decisions."

Hickman devised a platoon system, rotating five-man units each 10 minutes, and U of L wore out Georgetown 99-27 in the coach's first game. The 99 points were a school record that would stand until 1953, and the 72-point margin remains the school's most lopsided victory.

The Cardinals reeled off six more in a row, and by season's end U of L had won 16 of its 19 games.

On January 13, 1945, Louisville received a preview of big-time basketball when it participated in part of a doubleheader at the Jefferson County Armory. In the opener the Cards buried Berea, and later George Mikan's 30 points helped DePaul beat Western Kentucky handily. The twinbill attracted 5,681 fans and the event was deemed such a success that U of L's home game with Western in February was also moved to the Armory.

At the end of the season, the Cardinals were invited to play in the National Association of Intercollegiate Basketball Tournament (NAIB) in Kansas City but had to decline because of the wartime travel restrictions.

THE 1945-46 SEASON With his five top players returning for the second time around, Hickman followed suit his second year, winning 22 of 28 games. Again, Hauptfuhrer and Ed Kupper were the leading scorers.

One of the most noteworthy events took place on November 28, when the Cards hosted Kentucky Wesleyan at the 3,000-seat Male High Gym. For the first time ever, a U of L game was broadcast by a local radio station.

Frank Epley tries to find a teammate during a 1946-47 practice session.

"Peck Hickman is the man largely responsible for the winning ways of the Red and Black basketball team," wrote Roger Madison, sports editor of *The Cardinal*, the U of L student newspaper. "Before Hickman took over the reigns of the Shipp Street school's cage squads, U of L was usually mediocre at best. Since the pudgy and jovial mentor acquired the helm, the Cardinals have made winning a habit."

With the war now over, Hauptfuhrer was free to transfer at the end of the season, and he finished his college basketball career at Harvard.

"Naturally, getting a Harvard degree is the ultimate in education," he said, "but my fondest college memories lie in Louisville."

THE 1946-47 SEASON With the defection of Hauptfuhrer and the loss of Don Kinker and Ace Parker, 1946-47 became a year of transition. For starters, Frank Epley returned after completing his military stint. As for newcomers, Hickman landed Jack Coleman, Johnny Knopf, and Deward Compton, and all would play instrumental roles as the Cardinals completed their third consecutive winning season during the Hickman era, winning 17 of 23 games.

Hickman now even had an assistant coach, Dave Lawrence, and together they began recruiting a team that would bring Louisville to national prominence.

Louisville opened with an embarrassing 68-60 loss to Kentucky Wesleyan at the Armory. After the game, Hickman was livid. "We're not only going to beat Georgetown in our next game, but we're going to hold them under 40 points," he promised. "Otherwise, there'll be hell to pay!" His players got the message and Georgetown fell 76-40.

A week later in another home game, a crowd of 6,000 watched the Cardinals, 18-point underdogs, stun Western 60-52 with Kenny Reeves scoring 15 points and Coleman 14. The Hilltoppers more than avenged the loss a month later, winning 77-34 in Bowling Green. "Louisville made a mole hill out of a mountain before 6,000 awestruck fans," wrote sportswriter Tommy Fitzgerald.

THE 1947-48 SEASON (NAIB CHAMPIONS)

It was in the summer of 1947 that Hickman first became acquainted with

Because the team was now winning and drawing larger crowds, Peck Hickman convinced the new U of L president, Dr. John Taylor, that a larger playing facility was necessary. Consequently, the Cards ironed out an agreement to lease the Jefferson County Armory.

Cover of 1948 NAIB Tournament program.

NATIONAL INTERCOLLEGIATE BASKETBALL CHAMPIONSHIP TOURNAMENT

OFFICIAL PROGRAM

1947 ALL-AMERICAN TEAM

PRICE 25¢

MARCH 8, 9, 10, 11, 12, 13, 1948

MUNICIPAL AUDITORIUM · · KANSAS CITY, MO.

Billboard outside the Ballard Flour Mill plant in Louisville.

"The Baron," Adolph Rupp of Kentucky. Initially the two coaches met while Hickman was pursuing his master's degree at UK. Rupp was always happy to offer advice, but as soon as Hickman mentioned a possible game between Louisville and Kentucky, Rupp made it known that he was not in favor of such a match.

"Coach, we'd like to bring our team up here and play you," Hickman suggested. "Would you be interested in playing us?"

"Now Hickman, why do you want to go and mess up a good thing?" Rupp said. "You're gonna have a good team and probably go to the NIT, and we're gonna have a good team and go to the NCAA. By gawd, why should we take a chance and screw it up for one of us?"

Unknown to either coach, though, the first meeting between Kentucky and Louisville since 1922 would take place before the 1947-48 season was over. And although it would not be pleasant for Louisville, it would bring down the curtain on Hickman's most successful season yet.

NO QUALMS ABOUT SHOOTING U of L opened fast, running off nine straight victories. One of those wins was a come-from-behind 56-55 victory at Eastern Kentucky. With just under a minute to go and Eastern up by a point, Coleman grabbed a rebound, passed to Glenn "Ish" Combs, and the Cards were off on a three-on-one fast break. A lay-up that would put the visitors ahead for keeps seemed all but certain. But Combs, who often said he never met a shot he didn't like, stepped over the midcourt stripe and unleashed a two-hand set shot. Fortunately for both Combs and U of L, the ball swished through the nets and Louisville won the game.

Perhaps Louisville's biggest rival in the 1940s was Peck Hickman's alma mater, Western Kentucky. Second from right is Western's Gene Rhodes, who went on to become a standout high school, college and professional coach.

"Combs, what the hell were you thinking about?" Hickman inquired afterward.

"Well, Coach, I figured I was due," Combs shrugged.

The Cardinals took a 21-4 record into the KIAC Tournament at the Armory and gained the final round by handily disposing of Union, Transylvania, and Murray State. This set up a third match with Western, which by now was 24-1 and ranked third nationally behind Kentucky and North Carolina State. The Hilltoppers already had beaten U of L 71-44 and 77-55.

With a minute to go, Combs sank a set shot from beyond 20 feet to give the Cards a 62-61 lead. Then U of L intercepted a pass and tried to put the ball in the deep freeze. But with the final 10 seconds ticking away, Western's Duck Ray raced in for a clean swipe of a Louisville pass. He drove to the other end and softly laid it in a split second before the final horn sounded.

The Cardinals had little time to be downcast. Because of their outstanding 24-5 record, they were invited to the 32-team National Association of Intercollegiate Basketball Tournament in Kansas City's Municipal Auditorium. This time they eagerly accepted the bid. Meanwhile, Western entered the NIT as the team to beat and Kentucky was favored to win its first NCAA crown.

Louisville had its sights aimed beyond the NAIB because the winner would go to the Olympic Trials at Madison Square Garden in New York. Here, the NAIB

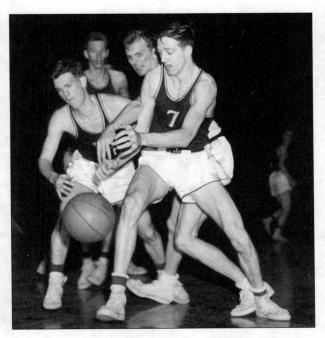

Roy (Button) Combs
and Lum Edwards
go for a loose ball
during a 1949 game.

champion would join the NCAA champion and runner-up and the NIT champion in one four-team bracket of the Olympic Trials. The other bracket would consist of the powerful AAU champion and runner-up, and the YMCA champion and runner-up.

En route to Kansas City, the Cardinals stopped in St. Louis for a game with Washington University. U of L hung on, 48-46, when Johnny Knopf grabbed a loose ball and drilled a buzzer-beating set shot.

The first opponent at Kansas City for U of L was South Dakota, and Louisville won a close one 63-60 in a game in which the Cards looked unimpressive. "We won the game but it seemed like every player they had was 6-foot-3 and weighed about 220 pounds," said Coleman, who led the winners with 17 points. "They banged us around pretty good."

Two nights later, Coleman and Compton collected 18 points each and Knopf 17 as Louisville pulled the tournament's first major upset by beating Emporia, 82-66. Meanwhile, defending champion Marshall was dethroned by San Jose State.

Next was a quarterfinal game with favored Beloit, which at 22-2 was rated as one of the teams to beat. Beloit's leading scorer was Johnny Orr, later to become head coach at Michigan and Iowa State. U of L, however, met the challenge and won 85-76. Orr scored 31 points while Combs paced Louisville with 19.

CARDINALS QUIZ

3. What was the last team from Kentucky that Louisville defeated in an NCAA Tournament game?

Jack Coleman, who wound up making the NAIB all-tournament team, gets the tip to start the second round game against Emporia.

The U of L vs. Indiana State NAIB game was Coach John Wooden's last game for the Sycamores. The following year, he was named head coach at UCLA, where he would remain through 1975 and win more national championships than any other coach in history. One of those who recommended him for the post at UCLA was Peck Hickman.

This moved the Cardinals into the semifinals for a third meeting against Xavier. Louisville had to rally from a 32-27 halftime deficit to beat the Musketeers, 56-49. In the other semifinal, John Wooden's Indiana State Sycamores nipped Hamline 66-65 in overtime, setting up a championship game on March 13.

When the Louisville team arrived for the big game, Hickman was going over strategies when one of the players burst into the locker room out of breath. "Coach, we got troubles."

"What?" Hickman asked.

"I can't find that little guy! Where are you s'posed to sit?" The player was referring to C. R. Dudley, a superstitious native of Kansas City who had taken a liking to the Cards. Before each tournament game, Dudley told Hickman where to sit on the bench. Failure to do so, Dudley warned, could mean defeat. Four straight times he had been right, and with a possible championship only a couple of hours away, Hickman wasn't about to mess with the supernatural.

Shortly before taking the floor against the Sycamores, there was a knock on the door of the U of L dressing room. Dudley had arrived. Two hours later, with Hickman sitting in the third seat from the left, Louisville defeated Indiana State, 82-70, to win its first national title.

But the season was not yet over for Hickman's team, which by now had compiled a team record 29 victories against only five losses. "It was tough on us every step of the way," Hickman told the cheering crowd. "We played five games in six days and, believe me, these weren't easy games. Now I'm going to give them a day or two off and then it'll be back to work."

While the team tried to concentrate on basketball, fans and reporters were still feasting on the accolades from Kansas City.

"Three things that happened in Kansas City were indications that the University of Louisville is now a big-time member of college basketball," wrote *Louisville Times* columnist Buck Weaver. "First, Coach Hickman has been offered a major coaching job. Second, Louisville has been invited to play in a major tournament in Los Angeles. Third, more than 4,000 people were on hand to greet the team when they arrived at Central Station last night."

"How did you know about the Texas job?" Hickman later asked Weaver. "Well, don't worry. I'm not going."

The tournament in Los Angeles also failed to materialize, but the crowd on hand to greet the team at the train station was very real.

OLYMPIC TRIALS Now Hickman and the Cardinals set their sights on New York City and the Olympic Trials. And even more exciting news came a week later when the pairings for the eight-team tournament were announced. They included Louisville vs. Kentucky.

Kentucky, which had won its first NCAA championship by beating Baylor at Madison Square Garden on March 23, was being called in the New York press "probably the greatest college team of all time." But the AAU champion Phillips Oilers of Bartlesville, Okla., were tagged the team to beat overall.

Left to right are Johnny Knopf, Kenny Reeves, Gil Waggoner, Glen (Ish) Combs and Roy (Button) Combs.

"Sure, Kentucky's good, but we're not going up there just to hold the score down," Jack Coleman said. "We aim to beat 'em." Hickman opted for a man-to-man defense against Kentucky's Fabulous Five. Coleman would guard Alex Groza, Reeves would have to handle Ralph Beard, Combs would be on Cliff Barker, Knopf on Kenny Rollins and Compton on Wah Wah Jones.

Some 2,000 Kentuckians, including Lieutenant Governor Lawrence Wetherby and Louisville Mayor Charles Farnsley, made the trip to the Big Apple and four Louisville radio stations broadcast the game.

Louisville took an early five-point lead but Kentucky came back and scored an easy 91-57 win. The Wildcats then defeated Baylor to reach the championship, which they lost to the Oilers, 53-49.

To this day, Reeves firmly believes that originally Louisville and Kentucky were not supposed to meet in the first round of the Olympic Trials. "I had heard that the pairings for that tournament had the NCAA runner-up playing the NAIB champion and the NIT champion playing the NCAA champion," Reeves said. It is his contention that the powers-that-be in New York did not favor having two teams from Kentucky playing for the college championship.

Dee Compton displays the NAIB trophy as the victorious Cards return to Louisville.

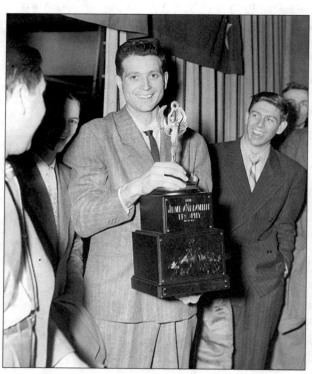

Ish Combs (left) and Kenny Reeves flank movie star Joan Leslie during a meeting in 1949.

THE 1948-49 SEASON Of the starters off the NAIB winners of 1947-48, only Deward Compton had been a senior. With the likes of Coleman, Knopf, the Combs brothers and Reeves returning, optimism for continued success was high.

Hickman, ready to take advantage of the national exposure the team had received, upgraded the schedule by including a four-game road trip into Pennsylvania and New Jersey and a home exhibition with the powerful Phillips Oilers.

But before departing for the East, where the Cards would take on Duquesne, Seton Hall, La Salle, and Westminster, they won a four-team midseason NAIB Invitational Tournament in Kansas City. And if this beefed-up schedule wasn't enough, U of L was also a charter member of a new conference. Instead of playing in the KIAC, the Cardinals joined the new Ohio Valley Conference, which included Eastern, Western, Murray, Morehead, and Marshall.

Another change was the addition of John Dromo as Hickman's assistant coach.

One anticipated change that failed to materialize was Hickman's dream of a regular-season encounter with Kentucky. U of L President John Taylor offered the Wildcats $10,000 to play a home-and-home series in 1948-49, but UK declined.

U of L finished 23-10 and was given an opportunity to defend its NAIB title but for the second time had to decline. This time the reason was money. "It cost us $900 last year and we just can't afford it," explained business manager Bo Clayton.

THE 1949-50 SEASON

THE 1949-50 SEASON After a one-year stand in the Ohio Valley Conference, Hickman decided the Cardinals could fare just as well as an independent. So, when the league voted to drop U of L in December 1949, it was no big deal to the Louisville coach.

"We were trying to upgrade our football schedule but couldn't do it against the OVC schools," Hickman explained. Another matter involved U of L's use of a reserve player in a game against Western. The OVC ruled the player was ineligible because of a transfer rule.

For the 1949-50 campaign, Hickman returned Ish and Button Combs, Kenny Reeves, and Lum Edwards and picked up Bob Lochmueller, a native of Tell City, Ind., who had transferred from little Oakland City College. The Cardinals won 16 of their first 18 games, including a season-opening double knockout in which they beat Kentucky Wesleyan, 69-44, and Georgetown College, 57-47, on the same night. "I don't think we'll try that again," said Hickman afterwards. "We started getting a little tired in the second game."

Lum Edwards practices on a pinball machine as Peck Hickman watches while the team waits to catch a train. Behind Hickman on the next machine is Ish Combs, who was elected posthumously to the U of L Athletic Hall of Fame in 1995.

NOSEDIVE On January 18, Louisville polished off Eastern Kentucky to run its season ledger to 16-2 and all seemed right with the world. But then the bottom dropped out. For one thing, Ish Combs, hampered throughout his career with knee problems, was finally wearing down. "Ish doesn't complain, but he made a lot of jumps as a paratrooper during the war, and his arches have

No, this isn't Swan Lake. Louisville's Kenny Reeves (13) battles Western's Johnny Oldham for a ball in a 1948 game at Bowling Green.

weakened," Hickman said. Lochmueller, Gil Waggener, and sophomore forward Bob Brown also were slowed by injuries. One who was not ailing was Reeves, who set a personal high with 32 points in a victory at Seton Hall.

The skid began with a 96-72 setback at Marshall. From there the Cardinals dropped eight of their last 14 to finish at 21-11. For the first time since Hickman's first year, U of L did not participate in a postseason conference or national tournament.

THE 1950-51 SEASON By the 1950s, just about all of the "patsies" were gone from U of L's schedule. With the Cardinals no longer bound to conference opponents, the 1950-51 agenda was Hickman's most aggressive yet.

Included was another trip east to meet Seton Hall and Villanova. There also were three Southeastern Conference teams: Mississippi State, Georgia Tech, and Tennessee. Then there were home-and-home series with North Carolina State, Xavier, and Dayton. And finally, a trip south for games with Memphis State, Tampa, and Miami.

"Bob Lochmueller is one of the best players in the country," Hickman boasted at the beginning of the season. "I wouldn't be afraid to use him anywhere." Backing up the 6-5 Lochmueller were Bob Brown (also 6-5) and guards Dick Robison and Bob Naber.

The Cards opened 4-0 at home, but it wasn't until they upset powerful Seton Hall and its giant 6-11 center, Walter Dukes, 60-58, that they first drew national attention. Even though Louisville lost to Villanova, 68-60, the following night, the team was still impressive. Especially Lochmueller, who scored 27 in that setback.

At the holiday break, U of L was 8-1 and Hickman was believing that he just might have a tournament contender. After beating Memphis State for the second time on January 13, he was sure of it. Now Louisville's record was 13-1. Four nights later, the roof caved in at

THE COMING OF BIG-TIME CHARLIE

Despite being well over 6 feet tall as a ninth-grader at Louisville's Barret Junior High School in the fall of 1949, Charlie Tyra wasn't really into sports. Admittedly, he did like basketball and had tried playing but just never had any success. However, a man named Junie Jones changed all that the year after he became the first football coach at Atherton High.

"Come to Atherton, totally dedicate yourself, and you can play football or basketball or both," Jones urged a small group of youngsters at Barret one day. Tyra was one of the kids in that group. "If you put everything into it I ask, you have a good chance of becoming a sports hero and the girls will be chasing you all over the place. But if you go to Male, St. Xavier, Flaget, or Manual and try to play, you'll just sit on the bench — you'll be lost in the crowd."

In the fall of 1949, Tyra accepted Jones' advice and enrolled at Atherton.

"When I arrived at Atherton, I was a beanpole," Tyra recalls. "I was tall but weighed only about 165 pounds. But then Junie Jones and Ralph Mills (the Atherton basketball coach) made me their special project." Every day at lunch, Tyra would eat in about five minutes and then it was off to the gym, where Jones would be waiting for him. At first, Jones would merely throw a ball against a wall and have Tyra go after it. Again and again and again. Then he would throw it against the wall but with one alteration. Instead of having Charlie merely catch the ball, Jones would tell him to keep batting it so it wouldn't hit the floor. This, Jones explained, was to develop a sense of timing.

In addition to these never-ending rebounding drills, there were tipping drills, figure-8 drills, dribbling drills, running drills — everything needed to improve the skills of a big man. Jones knew them all. He had learned them from Peck Hickman. By now, Hickman was periodically coaching clinics for local high school coaches, and

Dayton. Not only did U of L lose 68-61 but in the process it blew a 19-point lead. Afterward the Louisville coach, angered by the antics of a hostile crowd, vowed never to play in Dayton again. Louisville won its next four before dropping four of its last six regular-season games. A 19-6 slate might not be good enough for a tournament bid, U of L fans feared after a 72-66 loss at Toledo in the last game of the year.

But on March 12, not only did the Cardinals receive their first NCAA Tournament bid, Hickman informed his players that the first opponent would be Kentucky. It would be the first encounter with Rupp's Wildcats since the 1948 Olympic Trials, and the game would be played in Raleigh, N.C.

Unlike the previous meeting, Louisville gave tournament-favored Kentucky all it wanted. After trailing

Jones attended them all even though his job at Atherton was to coach football.

By the end of his junior year, it became evident that Tyra had a future in either basketball or football. John Dromo, by now well established as Hickman's assistant coach, was looking at him, as was Ed Diddle of Western Kentucky.

Charlie Tyra

But equally interested in Tyra was a football coach, Bear Bryant of Kentucky. Along the way, Jones not only had been successful in converting Tyra into a highly sought basketball player but also had found himself a football star.

"Bryant had me up to look at Kentucky sometime after my junior year and at that time, I was kind of leaning toward playing both sports in college," Tyra said. "Bryant introduced me to some of the players, like Babe Parilli, and he showed me Stoll Field, where Kentucky played its home games. Then he took me across the street to Memorial Coliseum to introduce me to Mr. Rupp."

Kentucky had just finished practice when Bryant introduced Tyra to Rupp, who grasped his hand. "C'mere, boy, I want to show you something," Rupp said in his Kansas twang. He took him to midcourt. "If you come here and play on this floor for me, you can be an All-American by the time you leave." But Charlie was not impressed.

In both his junior and senior years at Atherton, Tyra, relying primarily on a jump shot nobody could block, led the basketball team in scoring and rebounding. His senior year, he averaged over 20 points and made the *Courier-Journal* All-State team. A short time later, he decided to enroll at the University of Louisville.

Scoreboard at the old Louisville Armory.

44-40 at halftime, Louisville forged ahead, 59-54, on a lay-up by Brown. A few minutes later, with U of L still in front at 64-60, Kentucky's 7-foot center, Bill Spivey, fouled out. But substitutes Skippy Whitaker, Frank Ramsey, and Lou Tsiouropolous (pronounced Sha-ROP-o-lus) led a comeback that saw UK win, 79-68. Later in March, the Cats won their third national title.

"Louisville was one of the best teams we played all season," Rupp later said.

"Yeah, but we lost," Hickman groaned. But, he promised, "the next time we play them it will be different."

THE 1951-52 SEASON Perhaps one of the biggest things to happen at U of L had nothing to do with basketball, although the impact would be tremendous about a decade down the road. For the first time, African-American students were allowed to enroll. This resulted after Louisville agreed to absorb all-black Louisville Municipal College.

As for the basketball season, things couldn't have looked better for Hickman, who returned all of his starters from the 1950-51 NCAA squad: seniors Bob Lochmueller, Bob Brown and Bob Naber and juniors Dick Robison and Bill Sullivan. Newcomers included stars-to-be Chuck Noble of Akron, Ohio, and Corky Cox of West Point, Ky.

After watching Louisville crush Georgetown College 92-36 in the opener, losing coach Humzey Yessin, who had played for Adolph Rupp, gave his ex-mentor a call. "Coach, man for man I'd have to say Louisville is as good as any team in the country. I'd take their first nine or 10 players and take on any team, including UK."

Louisville completed its season by routing Xavier 101-87 with Brown getting 26, Noble 25 and freshman Frosty Able 14. Afterward, the Cards accepted a bid to the NIT in New York City and were paired against the strong Hilltoppers of Western.

"We hadn't had any luck in the past in getting an NIT bid," Hickman recalled. "Then I invited Ned Irish to speak at our basketball banquet. He was the one who ran Madison Square Garden. He wasn't a very good speaker, but he invited us to the NIT — finally!" On March 8, Gene Rhodes, a Louisville Male High product, led Western to a 62-59 win over Louisville, ending another successful U of L season at 20-6.

THE 1952-53 SEASON Hickman entered the season with mixed emotions. He had no impact seniors other than Dick Robison and Bill Sullivan, but with this young team, the future looked bright indeed.

Returning for his junior year was 6-4 forward-guard Chuck Noble, a double-figure scorer his sophomore year. Other starters included guard Corky Cox, 6-5 sophomore Vlad Gastevich and, before the season was over, freshman Phil Rollins. In time, Rollins would become one of the most popular Cardinals of the Hickman era.

Rollins, from Wickliffe in western Kentucky, was an outstanding long-range shooter with a high theshold of pain — important, because he suffered many injuries. He was also respected as a passer — a referee once decided that "the kid has to have eyes in the back of his head." Rollins, who had learned basketball by shooting through a makeshift hoop nailed to a shed in his backyard, was 10 years younger than his famous brother Kenny, a member of Kentucky's Fabulous Five in the late 1940s. Phil, an all-state player his junior and senior years at Wickliffe High, had every intention of following in big brother's footsteps and signing with Kentucky. But in the summer between his junior and senior seasons at Wickliffe, he became friends with Dromo and Hickman and changed his mind.

THE NIT U of L was paired against Georgetown University and came away with a 92-79 win. But in the second round, the Cards were ousted by Manhattan's Jaspers, 79-66 after falling behind 41-21 in the first half. Seton Hall went on to win the tournament.

The highlight of the year occurred at the Armory on March 2 when the Cardinals took on No. 1 Seton Hall, led by 6-11 All-American Walter Dukes. Louisville's stunning 73-67 upset win was on television — a rarity for the time — and it wound up as a photo feature in Life *magazine. Actually, the photos centered on a bench-emptying brawl at the end of the game. In Gary Tuell's book,* Above the Rim, *Louisville's Chet Beam described the fight this way: "Henry Brooks (of Seton Hall) hit Corky Cox with an elbow as the game ended. I walked over to Brooks and said, 'The game's over, let's not have any trouble.' As I started to walk away, I saw a fist coming. I ducked and it grazed me. The next thing I knew Chuck Noble charged Brooks and knocked him to the floor. Then players from both teams stormed the floor." Brooks said he swung at Beam but that another U of L player swung at him.*

THE 1953-54 SEASON Charlie Tyra was on the freshman team, but due to a rash of injuries actually played in 13 games with the varsity, which was highly unusual in this era. "Hickman and Dromo had this unbelievable threshold for pain," he remembers. It was during this season that Charlie began to develop a soft hook shot that in later years would become his trademark.

For almost two hours he would practice with the freshmen, coached by Dromo, and then Hickman would invariably demand that he work with the varsity. In practice, Hickman was demanding to the highest level. An infraction of any kind, such as a missed play, always meant laps around the gym and up and down the stairs.

A popular player in the early 1950s at Louisville was guard Corky Cox (3), shown here vying for a loose ball. Cox and Chuck Noble were co-captains of the 1953-54 team.

"Hurry back," Hickman would tell the guilty player.

With Tyra on board and 6-9 John Prudhoe ready to start at center, Hickman had plenty of size. Also, Noble and Cox returned as seniors.

From an 89-71 loss to Western on December 30 until a season-ending victory at Eastern on March 3, U of L won 14 of its last 17 to finish the regular season at 22-6. The Cardinals were extended their third consecutive National Invitational Tournament bid, and their first opponent was local favorite St. Francis of Brooklyn.

By holding Noble to 10 points and Rollins to just eight, St. Francis upset the Cardinals, 60-55. Hank Daubenschmidt, a 6-9 pivotman, kept Tyra in check while scoring 20 points and snaring 14 rebounds.

"How can you expect to win when you don't play?" Hickman fussed afterwards. "We just stood around." Next year, he hoped, would be different.

CARDINALS QUIZ

4. What well-known U of L player holds the record for most points in a single game?

THE 1954-55 SEASON Tyra made his presence known early in his sophomore year. Not only did he lead the team in scoring with a 14.7 average but he also averaged 13.6 rebounds for a team that compiled a 19-8 record and reached the second round of the NIT.

While the Cardinals proved to be formidable opponents for just about anyone, they had one major problem: winning the close ones. Most bitter were two overtime losses to archrival Dayton. There were two four-point setbacks to Marquette and an overtime loss at Eastern Kentucky in early February. The Cards were beaten only once by more than six points, and that was to Duquesne in the NIT.

"Next Year" Arrives

THE 1955-56 SEASON
(NIT CHAMPIONS)

On October 8, 1955, "next year" came to Brooklyn as the Dodgers finally beat the Yankees in the World Series. Peck Hickman couldn't help but hope that this would be "next year" for his team. Four straight trips to the NIT were preceded by one to the NCAA, and the best Louisville had done was to advance one round.

Hickman was poised for what he was thoroughly convinced could be one of his best teams — and all had been winners. With Charlie Tyra in the middle, two strong guards in senior Phil Rollins and junior Jim Morgan, and three outstanding forwards in Bill Darragh, Herb Harrah, and Gerald Moreman, he had reason for optimism.

By now Tyra was a towering 6-8, yet he was only the third-tallest U of L player behind 6-10 Jerry DuPont and 6-9 Jim Hereen. Other members of the team included Dick Keffer, Roscoe Shackleford, Al Glaza, and Harold Pike. Keffer and Shackleford were natives of Hazard and both were known for their hustle.

A large crowd is on hand for this game in the smoke-filled Louisville Armory.

"If there was a fight somewhere after a game, you could bet that Keffer would be right square in the middle of it," Darragh said. "And the guy he was fighting usually didn't know it until it was too late because Dick always threw the first punch. It seemed like Dick was at his best around 3 o'clock in the morning."

Louisville opened on December 2 by clobbering Georgetown College, 72-46. After beating Murray and Wayne State, the team headed to Buffalo, N.Y., for a game with Canisius. U of L scored a routine 98-82 victory, and on the train back to Louisville that night, Tyra, who scored 38 points and grabbed 33 rebounds, had just dozed off in his Pullman berth when the curtain opened and there stood assistant coach John Dromo. "Charlie, you played a great game. But I want to warn you of this. Keep it in perspective and don't let down, because the Big Man (Hickman) thinks this can be a very special team that can go a long way. The chemistry's there, we've got all the tools. Just remember what I said and don't let up."

Until that moment, Tyra had not looked upon this team as special. "I didn't realize until after I graduated or maybe in my senior year what chemistry meant," Tyra said. "Every team doesn't have it; in fact, most don't. But we were the perfect mix. We all got along, we complemented each other and we had fun. That was a true team."

On February 13, Louisville took a 19-1 record up U.S. 42 to take on Xavier in Cincinnati. By now there was no question that Louisville was a force to be reckoned with. And there was no question that on this night and on this court the Cards would pick up their 20th win. However...

Two games between these teams the previous season had been wars, and this year would come the sequel to that fiery miniseries. The first game between the two in 1954-55 had taken place at Xavier, and the Musketeers won 76-70 in a game Louisville players felt had been "stolen" by the officials. When the teams played later at the Armory, Hickman left his starters in until the closing moments and Louisville won, 92-52.

This time it was Xavier that was clawing for vengance, and the Musketeers responded with what Tyra later called "a perfect game." Xavier, led by a 5-6 midget named Jimmy Booth, sizzled from everywhere in the first half and didn't cool down much in the second, winning 99-59. "Booth was so quick that at one point Morgan was chasing him and finally, in frustration, just pushed him to the floor," said Darragh. "After that, I really didn't know if we'd get out of there alive."

"Booth's first name might as well have been John Wilkes, the way he murdered Louisville last night," one Cincinnati writer reported.

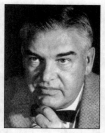

Bernard (Peck) Hickman

After the final meeting during the 1955-56 season with Eastern Kentucky (a two-point loss), Peck Hickman's wife waited patiently for him to emerge from the locker room. When he finally came out, she could tell immediately that he was as down as he had been all year. "Oh, c'mon, Peck," she said. "It's not all that bad. You still have the two girls and me." "Yeah," he snipped. "But right now I'd trade all three of you for three damn points."

Sporting a 21-2 record, Louisville went to Richmond for its third meeting of the year with Eastern Kentucky. Beating the Colonels in Louisville was one thing, but beating them in Richmond was quite another.

It didn't happen in 1954-55, and it didn't happen in 1955-56 either. Eastern Kentucky scored a controversial 86-84 triumph. After winning at Murray, 83-70, Louisville closed out its season by beating Xavier by the same score, holding Booth to nine points.

Now the Cards, 23-3, set their sights on another trip to Madison Square Garden for their fifth consecutive appearance in the NIT. They were seeded second, with Dayton — despite two losses to Louisville — getting the No. 1 seed in the 12-team field. Dayton's only other defeat had been at the hands of Duquesne.

This meant the Cards would receive a first-round bye and would meet the winner of a game between defending champion Duquesne and Oklahoma A & M. That turned out to be Duquesne, led by All-American Sihugo Green. Duquesne had been the team that had eliminated the Cards the previous season.

This time, despite a lackluster performance, Louisville won, 84-72, even though Green scored 24.

For the first time, the Cards were in the NIT semifinals, where St. Joseph's, which brought more than 1,000 fans, awaited. In the first half, Louisville was at its best and led 45-27. With Tyra getting 29 points and 20 rebounds, the final was 89-79, setting up a third game against Dayton, which defeated St. Francis, 89-58.

"Make it a five-point win for us," predicted Rollins. "That should be just about right."

"Five turnovers against these guys will probably beat us," Hickman warned Rollins and Morgan before the tipoff against Dayton. "We can't turn it over and expect to win."

The Flyers jumped out early and led 45-44 at the half. "During the break, Hickman gave us holy hell," Morgan said. "We thought we were doing pretty good, but he got us to thinking." At his home in Michigan, Kenny Rollins, Phil's older brother, nearly kicked in the screen of his television set when the tube went out shortly before halftime. Mumbling curses under his breath, Rollins stalked out of his house and down to the drugstore on the corner, where he caught the rest of the action.

In the second half, Morgan decided he would rather have the pain in his thigh than the uncomfortable padding he was wearing to protect a floor burn he had gotten in the semifinals. He threw the pad away and played an outstanding game the rest of the way. Meanwhile, Tyra began to dominate as 7-foot Bill Uhl and the Dayton players began to tire. Louisville pulled away and won, 93-80.

Afterward, as the team celebrated in the dressing room, Hickman joined in. Then he gathered his players

Students greet the champs on the oval in front of Grawemeyer Hall on Louisville's Belknap Campus.

A 100-car motorcade rolling down Preston Street toward Belknap Campus was led by this fire truck carrying the U of L basketball team.

around. "See, all those laps and all that hard work you've done this year paid off. I knew this team could be special, and you proved me right. Now you can go on with your celebration, but not too much because for you who will be back next year, I want you to know this. Everybody in the world will be gunning for you. You just made everybody's hit list."

Tyra, a Helms All-American, was unanimously voted the outstanding player of the 1956 NIT. His season average of 23.8 points per game remains the highest in U of L's history.

When the team landed at Standiford Field, the players were shocked when they stepped off the plane. A crowd estimated at 5,000 jammed the Lee Terminal. Several hundred had been turned away at the entrance, including some who had to give up their travel plans. "Mighty Moose, Mighty Moose," some yelled when Tyra emerged from the aircraft with a floral horseshoe around his neck.

THE 1956-57 SEASON It isn't often that a team ranked No. 1 in preseason polls can expect no pot of gold at the end of the rainbow, but that was the case at U of L despite a 21-5 season. The school was dealt a one-year probation from the NCAA after the 1955-56 championship year for overactive recruitment involving a 6-foot-5, 185-pound red-headed kid from New York City by the name of Don Goldstein.

Goldstein had come to Louisville purely by accident. The scouts were far more interested in his best friend and high school teammate, Alex Mantel. Goldstein offers this account of his first visit to Louisville: "I was raised by my grandmother, an uneducated woman who had come to America 40 years earlier and never left her little neighborhood in New York. It was a terrible area of Brooklyn, and if you went in there now you would find a ghetto. You'd have to carry a gun to survive. Even then it was tough, and my grandmother wouldn't let me go anywhere. Scouts came by from Villanova, Temple, and New York University, and they would try to get me to come visit their campuses, but she wouldn't let me go.

"Then Alex came by one day and said a scout from Louisville (Dromo) had watched us play and wanted us to come down. My grandmother, who didn't have a clue where Louisville was, relented this time since Alex was going. She thought it was some place close to New York City."

As freshmen in 1955-56, Mantel and Goldstein got caught up with Louisville's best team, the NIT champions. "We were so small compared to those guys, Tyra, DuPont. And they were great. No question that '55-56 team put Louisville on the map in basketball."

Street and Smith's ranked the Cards No. 1 in its preseason rankings as did several other polls.

Even though ineligible for postseason play, Charlie Tyra's senior year did bring some memorable events for U of L. After winning five of their first seven, including a 10-point victory over Notre Dame in their first game at Freedom Hall, the Cards captured the first Bluegrass Invitational. This tournament also was played at Freedom Hall, but all remaining home games were at the Armory.

Tyra ended his career with 1,728 points and 1,617 rebounds. The latter is still a record at U of L.

THE 1957-58 SEASON The year after Tyra graduated, Hickman suffered through his worst season in all of his 23 years at Louisville. A winning record of 13-12 was salvaged only because of home victories in the last two games over DePaul and Eastern Kentucky.

If there was a highlight to the year, it was probably at the postseason team banquet when it was announced that the surprise guest speaker would be Kentucky's Adolph Rupp. "You might not believe it, but Peck did a good rebuilding job," Rupp told a packed house at the Kentucky Hotel. "Don't be surprised if he doesn't turn this thing back around next year." In Freedom Hall, Louisville had won 12 of 14 and drew an average crowd of 5,116. But in 12 road games, the Cards beat only Iona.

The 1956-57 season marked U of L's first appearance in spacious Freedom Hall. After the Jefferson County Armory, Freedom Hall seemed overwhelming. Fans found the 18,000 seating capacity not only too big but inaccessible. The Armory, which comfortably housed around 7,000, had seemed ideal. Games there were community affairs. Freedom Hall, fans argued, deprived them of this aspect. Somehow, the crowds seemed larger and more intimidating to the opposition at the Armory and, for those who didn't want to drive, it was conveniently located downtown, right on the bus route. Yet Peck Hickman had fought hard for the move. Someday, he predicted, "We'll fill this place." But it would be a decade before the Cards would average 10,000 spectators a game.

THE 1958-59 SEASON (FINAL FOUR)

On the morning of the return match with Xavier, The Courier-Journal gave the Cardinals a ray of hope. "In 1956, U of L won the NIT with a record of 26-3," an article stated. "One of those losses was a 40-point thrashing at Xavier. But in the last game of the regular season, the Cardinals avenged that loss. If Louisville wants to be in a postseason tournament in 1959, history had better repeat itself."

On opening night, the 6-5 Don Goldstein would be one of two seniors in the lineup. He would start at forward, joined by 6-5 sophomore forward John Turner of Newport, Ky.; 6-2 senior guard Harold Andrews of Terre Haute, Ind.; 6-0 junior guard Roger Tieman of Covington, Ky.; and 6-11, 235-pound sophomore center Fred Sawyer, who had originally enrolled at Toledo but changed his mind. The only other senior on the team was another New Yorker, 6-2 Alex Mantel, but the bench looked fairly strong with junior forward Joe Kitchen and several promising sophomores.

Goldstein would be the "go-to guy" because he always seemed to have a real savvy for what lay ahead. "Hey, a pick's coming," he might warn a teammate. Goldstein was an outstanding passer, rebounder, and shooter. But in Hickman's words, "he needs to score more this year." Much was also expected of Turner, a quiet individual who Hickman felt could become one of the best forwards Louisville had ever produced.

By the end of the season, Hickman's most surprising player was possibly Sawyer. "He was a big, skinny, timid kid at the beginning of the year," Hickman said. "Then (U of L football coach Frank Camp) talked me into letting him help Fred in the weight room. By March, he was the best bench presser on the team, and in the games at the end of the year, he began dominating the boards."

The season-opener was against little Georgetown College, an NAIA school whose players looked upon the Cardinals as "giants." In spite of the fact that the Tigers returned most of their players from a team that had finished fourth in the 1958 NAIA Tournament in Kansas City, U of L viewed the inaugural 1958-59 contest as "no problem." But Hickman had scouted the Tigers in their first three games and knew the opener would be no blowout.

"I think Peck was a little concerned because we had already played those three games and this was his team's opener," Georgetown's coach, Bob Davis, would later theorize. The attendance that night was 3,893, but the real noisemakers were 250 fans from Georgetown.

Louisville took an early lead but could never really pull away and by halftime had allowed the visitors to forge ahead, 39-37. When it was over, Georgetown had won, 84-78, sending its fans pouring onto the playing floor in celebration. Someone handed sophomore star Corky Withrow a pocket knife, and as his teammates hoisted him on their shoulders, he snipped down one of the nets.

"It was the biggest win in our history, and even today I look back on it as one of the top feathers in my hat, and that includes the years when I coached at Auburn," Davis reflected.

Hickman would one day describe that loss as "the best thing that could have happened to us that year." With the Georgetown game serving as a wakeup call, Louisville returned to its home floor the following Saturday and promptly upset Georgia Tech's Engineers and their heralded sophomore, Roger Kaiser, 71-57. This was Hickman's eighth regular-season victory in eight tries against Southeastern Conference teams.

On December 8 came Louisville's first road trip, to Peoria, Ill., to face Bradley University. "They had this thing they called a gym, but really it looked more like a quonset hut and it was five below zero outside," said Buddy Leathers, a reserve guard. "The building was all metal and it was the noisiest place I'd ever been in. And Bradley had this player named Bobby Joe Mason, one of the few black players we faced that year. It seemed like he could do anything he wanted to against us. Our shooting against their zone defense in the gym that night was as cold as the temperature was outside." The final was 78-48.

On January 3, U of L took a 5-6 record to Cincinnati to take on Xavier. Two of the Musketeers' stars were from Louisville. They were Hank Stein, the NIT's Most Valuable Player in 1958, and Joe Viviano. The Musketeers also had a center named Rich Piontek, who was considered slightly better than his older brother Dave, by then in the National Basketball Association.

Louisville never had a chance. Xavier won 98-66 with Viviano scoring 22 and Stein 21. "Bradley beat us by 30 and Xavier by 32," Hickman said. "This better not happen again!"

"Listen to him, guys," Goldstein said after Hickman stormed out of the locker room. "We get Xavier and Bradley at our place in a couple of weeks, and I guarantee we're going to take care of both of 'em."

After beating a physical Eastern Kentucky team, 86-75, Goldstein and his mates prepared for their revenge. First was Xavier on January 10, and three nights later Bradley would invade.

Louisville made good on Goldstein's guarantee. First, the Cards edged Xavier, 70-66. They did the same to Bradley, winning 79-66. At last, U of L was above .500 at 8-7.

However, on January 17 Louisville dropped back to the break-even mark when it lost at Saint Louis, 69-68. Saint Louis was led by Bob Ferry, whose son Danny would become a star at Duke. During the second half,

Louisville arrived at the Mideast Regional semifinals one day early. That evening, Peck Hickman and John Dromo were to participate in a press conference for coaches and their assistants. "Now, I'm leaving you seniors in charge of supper plans," Hickman said. "Just order within reason and be sure to give me the bill." The players, accustomed to ham and roast beef sandwiches on the road, decided to go for it. Steak, baked potato, corn on the cob, apple pie, the works. Dromo, who returned ahead of Hickman, was infuriated. "You guys have to beat Kentucky now because when the Big Man sees this bill he's gonna kill all of you and then fire me!"

CARDINALS QUIZ

5. What well-know U of L players share the record for most points (26) in a half?

some Saint Louis students slipped behind mascot Richard Dyson and managed to rip off his coveted Cardinal Bird head. Enraged, Dyson started for the stands, where other students began passing the head one to another, just out of his grasp. The game stopped momentarily as ushers made a futile attempt to restore order. Dyson and the ushers were soon joined by security guards and police and finally, after a brief scuffle, the head was retrieved intact.

A week later, the Cards resumed their heated rivalry with the visiting Dayton Flyers. On this night, Louisville won easily, 76-59. It was Dayton's worst defeat to that point in the series, and Louisville drew its largest regular-season crowd of the year, 8,401.

A trip to Milwaukee for a game against Ed Hickey's Marquette Warriors was another matter. Marquette had a strong team, led by Don Kojis, who was destined for a career in the NBA, and Walt Mangum, who one day would become an Olympic high jumper. The Warriors scored a four-point victory and Louisville's tourney hopes now appeared bleaker than ever.

After trailing by a point at halftime, Louisville presented Hickman with his 300th victory by plastering Florida Southern, 88-57, in the only game the Cardinals played at the Jefferson County Armory that season.

On February 7, a long-awaited doubleheader took place at Freedom Hall that was originally supposed to include two superstars. The dream match, billed years in advance, was to pit Western Kentucky against West Virginia and its All-American, Jerry West, in the opener. Louisville was to play Kansas in what would have been Wilt Chamberlain's senior year for the Jayhawks.

Chamberlain, however, opted for a career with the Harlem Globetrotters after his junior year and by then had taken his act to the NBA. The Louisville-Kansas game remained, but Army replaced West Virginia as Western's opponent when the date of the Mountaineers/Hilltoppers game was changed to another night.

Although the Louisville fans were denied an opportunity to see the two All-Americans, U of L did defeat the Jayhawks, 82-74, and by doing so may have wrapped up an at-large berth in the NCAA Tournament. At least Hickman must have thought so. A few days later, Louisville received an invitation to play in the NIT. After a discussion with team members, he reported to President Philip Davidson. "Sir, we talked it over and we've decided to wait for an NCAA bid." Such a wait could be risky, Hickman knew, but he and Davidson agreed that it was the right decision.

U of L closed out its season by winning five of its last six — including a "payback" win over Marquette, 68-55 —

to gain an at-large spot in the NCAA's Mideast Regional.

The first opponent was Eastern Kentucky, champion of the Ohio Valley Conference. The game would be played March 10 at the University of Kentucky's Memorial Coliseum, and to the winner would go a trip to the Mideast Regional semifinals in Evanston, Ill., where Southeastern Conference representative Kentucky would be waiting.

In his *Louisville Times* column, The Press Box, veteran sportswriter Dean Eagle predicted Eastern Kentucky would upset the Cardinals. "If (Kentucky coach) Adolph Rupp thinks it would be humiliating losing to Louisville, think how he would feel if he lost to Eastern Kentucky? He just might. Eastern appears to be that good." Led by Goldstein's 25 points and with a crowd of 10,500 on hand, Louisville proved Eagle wrong and won, 77-63. Taking notes were five UK scouts and Coach Rupp.

Kentucky was established as a 10-to-12-point favorite against Louisville, which would be playing with a lame center. The 6-11 Sawyer severely fractured a toe on his right foot in the game with Eastern Kentucky and was listed as a doubtful starter.

John Turner (22) battles UK's Don Mills for a rebound while Kentucky's Dickie Parsons (51) looks on.

Fans give the U of L players a victory ride after 76-61 upset win over UK.

Although the Wildcats were the defending NCAA champs and were ranked second in both The Associated Press and United Press polls with a 23-2 record, they had received a bid to the NCAA Tournament only because SEC champ Mississippi State turned down the chance. The Starkville school's policy was not to participate in any tournament in which a rival team had black players on its roster.

LOUISVILLE VS. KENTUCKY For years, Kentuckians dreamed of such an engagement, yet since the 1920s only twice had it become a reality.

The game served as the opener of a doubleheader, with Big Ten champion Michigan State meeting Marquette, located only 70 miles from Evanston, in the second game. Long before the 7:30 tipoff of the U of L-UK game, McGaw Hall was jammed to capacity with 9,200 fans.

"To stop Kentucky you have to stop Johnny Cox and Bill Lickert." That, Hickman knew, was the key to victory. "I think the only way to stop Cox and Lickert is to shut down their guards because that's where they're weakest," he emphasized to his players. "We pick the guards up at midcourt and don't give them a thing.

Andrews, I want you on Lickert. Stick with him like glue!" Normally, Hickman followed his pregame strategy session with a pep talk, but this time the emotion was too much. He turned that task over to the volatile Dromo. "I sat there and listened to John talk, and I could feel the goose bumps running up and down my spine and my arms," Goldstein recalled. "By the time he was through talking, I was literally scared to death."

"Peck Hickman has given us everything he possibly has to give," Dromo began. "This is our chance to give something back. I'm sure he would never tell you this, but Peck would gladly crawl the length of this floor in front of all those fans just to shake Mr. Rupp's hand if he could win this game. That's how much it means to him because he knows that if he beats Kentucky tonight, then Louisville never again will have to settle for being considered second best."

Dromo said much more, but to this day, those words stand forever embroidered in Goldstein's memory.

It was as though each half was a separate game. The Wildcats, as expected, jumped ahead early and with 9:07 left before intermission, seemed thoroughly in control, leading 27-12. Goldstein was still feeling the effect of Dromo's speech. "We were down 15 and I wasn't even sweating. Hell, I was too pumped up." He also remembers wondering how Sawyer was bearing up. Goldstein had had to turn his head upon hearing Sawyer cry out when they injected the foot with Novocaine. Goldstein then watched in awe as Sawyer crashed the backboard to snare a rebound away from Cox. Then, it really got strange. It was as though fate suddenly intervened.

"At one moment everything that could go wrong was going wrong, but suddenly it was as though the game came back to us," Goldstein remembers. From that point, U of L's hawking defense began to take hold and by halftime the margin was sliced to 36-28. Still, at intermission, Peck Hickman was fuming.

"You know what's beating you?" he seethed. "Those damn blue uniforms. You can beat this team if you forget all that 'Big Blue' tradition crap. But if you keep playing like this, you might as well join them and put on blue ones, too. And I'll tell you something else. You aren't picking up their guards like I told you to. From now on, I don't want to see any daylight between you and the man you're guarding. If I do, you're coming out of the game and you won't be going back in!"

U of L began the second half with a vengeance. Goldstein, Tieman, and Sawyer, who was still trying to ignore the flashes of pain in his foot, sparked the comeback that drew the Cards even at 42-42 with 15 minutes remaining. Tieman twice stole the ball from

CARDINALS QUIZ

6. *This player, who was a starter on Louisville's 1985-86 NCAA championship team, holds the record for appearing in the most games (145). Who is he?*

Kentucky Coach Adolph Rupp gives some advice to one of his players as Louisville surges from behind.

Bennie Coffman and converted lay-ups. The second time he was fouled, and the free throw tied the game. Kentucky never recovered.

Moments later, Louisville, backed not only by its own fans but also by those from Michigan State and Marquette, took the lead and won going away, 76-61.

Four U of L players scored in double figures that night. Goldstein had 19, Andrews 15 and Tieman and Turner 13 each. Lickert led UK with 16 points. Cox was limited to 10.

"You really laid the wood to us, boy," Rupp told Hickman and then walked away. Then Rupp found radio broadcaster Cawood Ledford. "Damnit, you wanna know what they did to us, Cawood?" Rupp drawled. "Why, they just beat the hell out of us and ruined a beautiful season."

Hickman tried to talk to reporters but was constantly interrupted by fans pounding him on the back. "We might've beaten 'em sooner if we'd had a chance to play 'em," he quipped.

In the dressing room, Sawyer forgot his fractured toe as he accepted congratulations from well-wishers. "This is just too good to be true. Now we've got to forget about this game, come down to earth and win tomorrow night. Then we'll be back home and we can beat anybody at Freedom Hall." Nobody was doubting him.

"Kentucky gave us a really good game," John Dromo told a Chicago writer. "Almost as good as Eastern did."

Later, through the paper-thin walls separating the two dressing rooms, U of L players could easily hear Rupp chastising his players. "You know what they're gonna be doing now?" he growled. "They're going out and they're gonna be eating T-bone steaks. You're gonna have hamburgers and you better be glad you're getting those!"

No single victory in his career gave Hickman more satisfaction. Anything else in 1959 would be icing. "When we played Kentucky in 1948 there was no chance," he said. "They were already at the finish line and we were just getting out of the gate. In 1951, I thought we had a shot, but they wore us down at the end. But in 1959, I knew we were ready to get the job done. UK had no idea how good we really were that year."

The following night, after pounding Marquette in the consolation game, the Kentucky players sat behind the U of L bench, offering the Cardinals their vocal support. Louisville, a four-point underdog, nailed down the Mideast title by upsetting Michigan State and its All-American, Johnny Green, 88-81.

What this meant was that U of L would be coming back home to Freedom Hall as a member of the Final Four. The opponent would be West Virginia and its All-

Celebrating players hold up two fingers, signifying the number of victories still needed for the national championship after U of L stunned Michigan State to win the 1959 Mideast Regional Tournament at Evanston. However, this would be the Cardinals' last win of the year.

American, Jerry West. The second game would pair the Midwest champion Cincinnati Bearcats, led by Oscar Robertson, against defense-minded California. Because it would be playing on its home court, Louisville was made a five-point favorite.

West Virginia's mascot, a Mountaineer armed with a hunting rifle, foretold the home team's fate when he aimed his weapon at the Cardinal Bird. That picture was printed the following week in *Sports Illustrated*.

West was on fire that night, especially in the first half when he scored 27 of his 38 points. John Turner's short jumper tied the score at 26-26, but then West and his mates went on a 22-6 run that put them in front, 48-32, at halftime. Louisville made one mild rally, cutting the deficit to 49-38, but the Mountaineers spurted ahead, 60-40. When it was over, West Virginia had won 94-79. As *The Courier-Journal* reported the next morning, "Cinderella came home a bit early from the ball last night." Also home was Cincinnati, which was upended by California's slowdown tactics, 64-58.

U of L completed its season at 19-12 by losing the third-place game to Cincinnati, 98-85, as Robertson tallied 39 points. In the championship game, Pete Newell's surprising Golden Bears, rated last among the four teams going in, upset West Virginia, 71-70, to win their only NCAA crown.

Goldstein became the first Louisville player selected to the All-Final Four team, joining West, Robertson and Cal's Darrell Imhoff and Dennis Fitzpatrick.

THE 1959-60 SEASON Joining the three starters returning

from the Final Four team were 6-7 forward Bud Olsen, who had set a scoring record the previous season with the freshmen, and guard Ron Rubenstein, who had been sidelined with academic difficulties.

The Cards got off to a 4-0 start to set up a Freedom Hall engagement with No. 1 Cincinnati and Oscar Robertson, who came into the contest averaging 43 points a game. Controversy brewed when Hickman learned that two Louisville radio stations had opted to broadcast games from the University of Kentucky Invitational instead of the Cincinnati-Louisville game. "Am I wrong about this?" he asked. "Didn't we BEAT Kentucky last year?" At the last moment, a third local station stepped in and provided the play-by-play.

Cincinnati won, 97-74, and Robertson did his usual thing, scoring 39 and grabbing 19 rebounds. Turner had 22 and Olsen 15 in a losing cause for Louisville.

On February 3, U of L defeated Kentucky Wesleyan to run its record to 12-5, and its fans were still optimistic about a possible NCAA Tournament bid. However, successive losses to Xavier, Marquette, and DePaul (the latter two at home) ignited a tailspin from which the team never recovered. The Cards finished 15-11.

A DYING WISH GRANTED

Among those in attendance at the 1959 regional was Mulley Goldberg, possibly U of L's biggest fan. Mulley wasn't a Louisville alumnus but had become involved the year before when his son, Murrell, played with the freshman team. By the time the freshman season was in full swing, Mulley was Cardinal red through and through. In fact, during a game at Campbellsville he had been one of the few Louisville fans in history to be whistled for a technical foul.

Now things were different for Mulley. He was dying of cancer, and in February a large portion of his lung had been removed. He could only listen to the games on radio. But after the win over Eastern Kentucky made it a certainty that Louisville was going to play Kentucky, Mulley somehow mustered the strength to make the trip.

When Dr. Harry Gold offered to transport him to Evanston in his big Lincoln and watch over him during the game, it was as though his prayer had been answered. After the game, as Louisville celebrated on the court, U of L player Don Goldstein looked up into the crowd and saw two ushers lifting Mulley out of his seat. They carried him through the mob of fans onto the floor, and Goldberg, tears running down his face, told Goldstein: "You know, Don, you gave me one last thrill and I want to thank you so much," he said. "I felt like maybe you were playing for me out there." Less than a month later, Mulley died.

7. Louisville's longest winning streak is 18 victories in a row, set during the 1979-80 championship season. What is the record for consecutive losses?

THE 1960-61 SEASON For Kentuckians, the 1961 Mideast Regional at Freedom Hall was about as close to a "dream field" as you could ask for. The undefeated, top-ranked national champions, Ohio State, surrounded by three Kentucky schools. And for a few fleeting moments, it appeared that one of college basketball's great upsets just might happen.

Fred Taylor's highly favored Buckeyes were once again led by 6-10 All-American Jerry Lucas and future NBA star John Havlicek. On the bench was an often-used guard, Bobby Knight. Representing the Southeastern Conference was Kentucky, led by Cotton Nash. U of L and the Morehead State Eagles, co-champions of the OVC with Western Kentucky, completed the dynamite field. Ah, but that's getting ahead of the story.

With Fred Sawyer and John Turner the mainstays, along with junior Bud Olsen, Hickman couldn't help but envision a bright year, possibly even a championship. "After all," he mused, "if I could win the NCAA, then I would be the only coach to win an NAIB, an NIT, and an NCAA."

Louisville certainly looked formidable after demolishing Alabama, 90-53, in its season-opener at Freedom Hall. The Cards rolled to a 13-0 start and a No. 5 ranking. But the streak ended in a 78-70 loss to DePaul on January 14, and from there they went into a tailspin, losing seven of their last 13. Most notable of these defeats occurred in the next-to-last game of the season when Western Kentucky reversed an earlier 15-point loss by winning, 96-80.

Louisville was still invited to the NCAA and was seeded in the Mideast Regional preliminary round against Ohio University. To make matters even sweeter, the entire regional was to be held at Freedom Hall. U of L had set a school scoring record against the Bobcats during the regular season, beating them 117-84.

This time the team from Athens offered much more resistence. But Louisville broke away from a 30-30 halftime deadlock to win 76-70, setting up a second-round match with Ohio State.

A crowd that exceeded 18,800 jammed Freedom Hall to watch Kentucky knock out stubborn Morehead, 71-64, and then settled back to watch the mighty Buckeyes take on the home team. What they saw was one of the most exciting games in Freedom Hall's brief history.

For much of the way it appeared that Louisville — not Ohio State — would be meeting Kentucky for the Mideast championship. With Lucas hounded by as many as three players, the Buckeyes clung to only a 26-25 halftime lead. U of L took the lead and held it most of the second half. With 2:52 remaining, Turner's sixth straight free throw pushed the Cardinals' advantage to 54-49.

Then the Cards panicked. Three costly turnovers led to five straight OSU points and with 40 seconds left, the score was 54-54. At 18 seconds, Knight snared a teammate's rebound and Coach Taylor called time-out. His designed play didn't work exactly as planned, but Havlicek buried a jumper with four seconds left, giving Ohio State a 56-54 advantage.

Turner was fouled on the inbounds pass with just one second to go when Ohio State guard Larry Siegfried went for a steal. Turner made the first free throw but he missed the second. Sawyer tipped the ball to Turner, who got off a desperate 12-footer that skipped off the rim as the final horn sounded. A win over Morehead in the regional consolation gave Louisville a 21-8 mark.

THE 1961-62 SEASON With Turner, Sawyer, Howard Stacey, and Ron Rubenstein gone, Hickman found himself in a rebuilding state. The nucleus of this team would have to be senior Bud Olsen and perhaps sophomores John Reuther (6-9) and Ron Hawley (6-4).

U of L's major rival of the 1950s and into the early '60s was Dayton. In this 1962 game, Bud Olsen (13) is fouled by a Dayton player. Dayton won this game, 65–59.

It became evident early on that this would not be a banner year. A 30-point loss at No. 8 Duke in the third game and a one-point setback to St. Bonaventure in the championship game of the Bluegrass Invitational were the beginning. And if a home crowd exceeded 6,000 it was considered a good night.

Louisville lost four straight in February, then won five of its last six to finish a respectable 15-10. There was no postseason bid.

THE 1962-63 SEASON On February 11, it appeared almost a certainty that Hickman was going to suffer his worst season yet. That night the Cardinals were buried by Memphis State, 76-55, with Hunter Beckman hitting 13 of 19 shots and scoring 30 points for the winners. The loss was Louisville's fourth straight and lowered its overall record to a dismal 8-10.

But the Cards wound up 14-11, thanks to three overtime victories at Freedom Hall and road wins at Georgia Tech and Eastern Kentucky. Still, with the exception of 1957-58, it was Hickman's worst record.

THE 1963-64 SEASON No bands trumpeted the occasion and there were no banner headlines the following morning. The only mention was a fragment of a sentence in *The Courier-Journal*, buried deep in the game story. But on the night of November 30, 1963, a 6-foot-6 sophomore forward from Hazard, Ky., made University of Louisville basketball history.

His name was Sam Smith, long since forgotten in U of L basketball annals. He would later transfer to Kentucky Wesleyan and finish his playing days as a hero on a small-college championship team at that school. But his mere appearance that night had historical significance. When Smith entered the game against Georgetown College with 8:35 left in the first half, he became the first black player in a varsity game for U of L.

Actually, Louisville began the season with three black players, all sophomores. They were Smith, Wade Houston, and Eddie Whitehead. And before the game reached intermission that night, all three were on the court. But for history's sake, it was Smith who entered first. He finished with 11 points and Houston with 10. Whitehead failed to score as Louisville won, 113-82.

For several years, Hickman had wanted to bring black players into the Louisville fold and he considered several.

But before that decision was made, he sought the advice of U of L's only black faculty member at that time, Dr. Charles H. Parrish. Parrish had been the only faculty member retained in 1951 when U of L absorbed Louisville Municipal College, an all-black institution.

CARDINALS QUIZ

8. Once a starting guard for U of L, this player transferred to Cincinnati, where he became a regular on a Bearcat team that made the Elite Eight in 1996. Who is he?

Ground was broken in December 1963, for Crawford Gym, U of L's present practice facility. Left to right are Peck Hickman, Wade Houston (one of Louisville's first African American players) and U of L President Philip Davidson.

Although the football program had been integrated for many years with such standout players as Lenny Lyles and Ernie Green, Hickman was concerned. His basketball team made annual trips into areas that were still very hostile toward black athletes.

"Peck, we want to be careful about who we bring on board first," Parrish warned. "We want him to be a strong player, but he also has to be able to withstand all the abuse. In fact, if I were you, I would think about bringing in two or three at the same time. That way the burden wouldn't fall on one man's shoulders."

After cautious deliberation, Hickman, Dromo, and Parrish agreed on Whitehead, Houston, and Smith, who all came to Louisville as members of Dromo's freshman team of 1962-63.

Of the three, it was Houston who would have the biggest impact. In his senior year, both he and Whitehead would be starters and co-captains. And Houston would one day become a vital cog in the Louisville coaching system.

Dromo had warned each of the three that there probably would be incidents. "But I'll tell you this," he added. "When we go on the road as a team, we'll all stay together at the same hotel. We won't send the white players one place and you guys somewhere else. We're a team and you're an important part of that team."

Houston said Hickman and Dromo always kept their word. "There were instances on the road, like a taxi driver wouldn't pick us up or a restaurant wouldn't want to serve us. In cases like that, the whole team would just leave and we'd go somewhere else. I remember in my junior year we played in the Sugar Bowl basketball tournament in New Orleans, and some of the clubs along Bourbon Street wouldn't let us in. That was a big disappointment at the time. But then again, maybe they did the whole team a favor because we didn't have any business in those places anyway."

Louisville finished the 1963-64 season on a subpar note, reaching the NCAA Tournament only to be ousted by Ohio University, 71-69.

THE 1964-65 SEASON In the next two years, Hickman would land two of the most prolific high school players Kentucky had ever produced.

First was a machinist's son named Wes Unseld, a hulking 6-8, 240-pound center who had spearheaded Louisville Seneca to Kentucky state high school championships in 1963 and 1964.

Wes Unseld

"Wes had this big body and knew how to use it to his advantage," Hickman said. "He had an older brother at Kansas, and them and everybody else wanted him. But his parents wanted him close to home." Hickman recalled the many meetings he, Dromo, and the Unselds staged over the kitchen table at the Unseld home. "His dad once told us that if Wes got out of line to call him and he'd straighten his son out. But there is no doubt who was in charge of those meetings. Whenever we would have a conference at their house, we would sit at the kitchen table and Mrs. Unseld would take command." Unseld, who was listed as 6-8 but actually stood about 6-6, and 6-3 forward Fred Holden gave Dromo the nucleus of one of the most promising freshman squads Louisville had ever produced. So talented, in fact, that in a preseason scrimmage at Freedom Hall, Dromo's frosh beat the varsity, 87-86. Unseld had 33 points and 22 rebounds, and Holden contributed 30 points.

Although Unseld was now on board as Louisville's most prominent signee since Charlie Tyra, Hickman had to be more concerned with the immediate future. His top varsity point-maker would again be 6-7 John Reuther, now a senior. The club also had four other seniors in Tommy Finnegan, Dennis Clifford, Eddie Creamer, and Judd Rothman. Hickman also had Houston and untested sophomores Dave Gilbert and Joe Liedtke.

Louisville was ready for its debut into the Missouri Valley Conference, which at that time was still considered the best basketball league in the nation. After beating Georgetown and Marquette, U of L played its first MVC game December 12, losing at Cincinnati, 67-57. "Don't sell Louisville short in this league," Cincinnati Coach Ed Jucker warned later. "I was impressed with them."

It became apparent early in January that MVC games would be exciting. After losing by 14 at Tulsa, the Cards squeaked by North Texas, 70-68, in overtime and later upset Cincinnati, 82-80, on Liedtke's 20-footer late in the third overtime. On February 4 at Convention Center (formerly the Armory) Louisville avenged the earlier loss to Tulsa, winning 73-67. It was Hickman's 400th career victory.

Even with a so-so 15-10 record, Hickman could manage a smile at season's end. Wes Unseld was waiting in the wings.

THE 1965-66 SEASON After the 1964-65 season, Hickman landed another plum in Alfred (Butch) Beard of Hardinsburg. In 1964, Beard led Breckinridge County to the state championship game against Louisville Seneca. Unseld and the Redskins won that game, but Beard had been badly injured in Breckinridge County's semifinal victory and was unable to play. In 1965, he and

Coach Peck Hickman takes a snooze during a plane ride.

CARDINALS QUIZ

9. In 1951, U of L made its first NCAA Tournament appearance. Who was its first-round opponent?

Breckinridge County returned and won it all.

Beard thought seriously about attending the University of Kentucky, where he would become the first black player for Adolph Rupp. At the last minute, he decided to turn down the UK opportunity along with about 100 other offers in favor of becoming Unseld's roommate at Louisville.

As a sophomore, Unseld was the nation's No. 2 rebounder with an average of 19.4 per game, more than Louisville's other four starters combined. He shattered Oscar Robertson's 1957 Missouri Valley Conference rebounding record of 223 by hauling in 240 in 14 conference games. In all, he collected 505 over a 26-game schedule.

On offense, the big guy scored 518 points for an average of 19.9. He scored 35 against Bob Cousy's Boston College team in the NIT in a game U of L lost, 96-90, in three overtimes. As a result, Unseld was named to the All-MVC team.

THE 1966-67 SEASON Not in a decade had the future looked so promising. Unseld was entering his junior year as an All-America candidate, and he would be joined by Beard and several experienced, talented players.

In his sophomore year, Fred Holden had set a mark as the most accurate free-throw shooter in Louisville's history by making 97 of 114 attempts (85.1 percent). Known as a fierce competitor, this Youngstown, Ohio, native had been the team's No. 2 scorer behind Unseld. Hickman's plan was to flip-flop Holden and Beard between the forward and guard slots, depending on the situation.

"Holden was a very intelligent player," Hickman recollected. "He was a lot like Gerry Moreman had been and would ask a lot of questions. He could analyze a defense like nobody I ever saw and was probably the best free-throw shooter I ever coached."

Beard was moving to the varsity after averaging 25 points a game for the freshman squad. "Butch had trouble deciding if he wanted to play forward or guard, but he could handle either one like a pro," Hickman said.

CARDINALS QUIZ

10. In 1952, the Cardinals made their first NIT appearance. Who was their first-round opponent?

Louisville began in unusual fashion — its first eight games were at home. The Cards won all eight, rolling up scores of 107 against Southwest Louisiana and Tampa, 106 against LaSalle, 104 against Bellarmine, 99 against Georgetown, and 96 against Dayton. Only Southern Illinois and Saint Louis came within 10 points. After watching Beard score 34 against La Salle, Explorer coach Jack Heyer called him "the best player I've seen in two years."

U of L then ventured into Philadelphia for the Quaker City Classic, an eight-team holiday tournament. There the Cardinals beat Niagara, Syracuse, and Princeton to become the first non-Philadelphia team to win the tournament.

The streak reached 13 before Louisville finally stumbled, 53-50, at Southern Illinois on January 11. This was the first of four consecutive road games. After easy victories over Bradley and Dayton, the Cardinals suffered their second setback, 59-58, at Cincinnati on January 21.

Then, led by the explosive duo of Beard and Unseld, they began an eight-game winning streak, all over Missouri Valley opponents, including Cincinnati. This gave them a 23-2 record going into the final game of the season at Wichita State on February 25. Louisville had beaten the Shockers, 90-68, at Freedom Hall two weeks earlier.

Possibly the Cardinals were looking ahead to the NCAA Midwest Regional at Lawrence, Kan., but regardless, at Wichita they lost, 84-78. Yet neither players or fans seemed overly concerned.

"I guess you might say we arrived a year ahead of schedule," Hickman had told reporters before that game. He was referring to the fact that four of his starters would be returning.

The Midwest semifinals brought together three of the

Butch Beard of Louisville walks off the floor at Freedom Hall with a Florida State player. The FSU player at left is Dave Cowens, who later became a star in the NBA.

nation's top teams in Louisville, Houston, and Kansas, which would be playing on its home floor.

Louisville's first opponent, however, was unranked Southern Methodist, a veteran team that had won its third consecutive Southwest Conference crown.

Louisville's Wes Unseld takes a short jumper in a game with Memphis State.

With 10 minutes remaining, Louisville led, 64-61, thanks to a flurry of four baskets by sophomore Jerry King. But in the next breath, Unseld was whistled for his fourth personal foul. Yet the Cardinals padded their lead to 77-69. Then came big trouble.

SMU's Lynn Phillips connected twice from long range, one following two missed free throws by King. An SMU lay-up and now Louisville's lead was only 77-75. With less than a minute to play, a long jump shot by Bob Jones brought SMU even at 81-81.

With 58 seconds to play, Louisville called time-out. Forty-two seconds later, it called another, to design a play. The Cards worked for the winning shot, but with eight seconds left, Holden was tied up when he couldn't find an open man. SMU's Charles Beasley, two inches taller than Holden, batted the tip to his team's end of the floor, where it was scooped up by teammate Denny Holman. His lay-up just before the buzzer nailed down the upset for SMU.

"That was a devastating loss," Hickman said later. "That team could have gone a long way." The following night, U of L lost the consolation game to Kansas, 70-68. It was Hickman's final game.

During his 23 seasons, he had seen the Louisville program grow from obscurity to national prominence. He had won 443 games and lost 183 for a percentage of .708, ranking him among the nation's leading coaches.

Hickman had decided it was time to devote full time to his duties as athletic director. There was never a question who his successor would be.

CARDINALS QUIZ

11. Who holds the U of L record for most three-point goals?

'A Really Good Guy'

John Dromo

John Dromo came to the University of Louisville as an assistant football coach and golf instructor. A native of Cleveland, he later moved to Sharon, Pa., where he became known as the Ozark Ike of his day, playing virtually every sport.

It was at John Carroll University that Dromo learned that the fast break could be the most important part of college basketball. He also learned that the one-hand shot could be far more accurate than the popular two-handed bombs that delighted crowds in that era. "I saw Hank Luisetti score 50 points one night shooting that one-hander, and I'd never seen anything like it," Dromo recalled. "I went to practice the next day and it was amazing. But my coach would have nothing to do with it. He told me my ass would be back on the bus to Sharon if I ever used it in a game."

After graduating in 1939, Dromo began his career coaching a girls' team at St. Francis DeSales, a new high school in Newark, Ohio. "I was the coach until one day

Princeton's Chris Thomforde is outnumbered by three Louisville players in a scrap for a rebound. The Louisville players are Wes Unseld (31), Jerry King (holding ball) and Butch Beard (14).

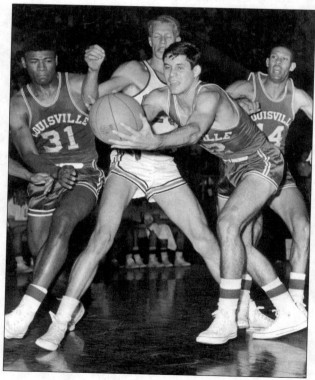

one of my girls fell down during a game," he is quoted as saying in Gary Tuell's book, *Above the Rim*. "She was a big girl, well put together, you know. All girl basketball players tend to be top-heavy, and this one was more so than most. Anyway, that makes it hard for them to keep their balance.

"So she went in for a lay-up and just fell over backwards. It knocked the wind out of her, so I ran out there like any coach would and put my hands under her waist and lifted her up to help her breathe. She had on this blouse with two buttons. Well, when I raised her up the buttons popped off. There I was holding this girl in my arms and the buttons were gone from her blouse. About that time, one of the nuns came running down from out of the stands and said maybe I should just coach the boys."

Later, he returned to John Carroll to coach part-time as a volunteer. But in the fall of 1942, he came down with rheumatic fever. "I tried to go into the Navy after that but they turned me down me because of an irregular heartbeat," Dromo said. "So maybe my heart was bad even way back then."

Instead of entering the military, Dromo moved to

John Dromo

Cincinnati, where he became assistant basketball and baseball coach at St. Xavier High School. He began in February 1943, at a salary of $260 per month. But after only two weeks, he was given the head coaching job in both sports. The first thing he did was to kick the seniors off the basketball squad. "They were too big, fat, and out of shape," he explained.

Under Dromo, St. Xavier was 32-4 in football and 82-10 in basketball. He left in May 1947 and settled in Louisville, at Male High School. There he became an assistant football coach under Nick Denes. To earn extra money, he officiated basketball games. One coach who was impressed with his officiating was Peck Hickman, who offered him "whatever games of ours you want" at $25 apiece. Dromo held out for $35. Neither Dromo nor Hickman would budge.

Peck Hickman grimaces from the Louisville bench. Next to Hickman is John Dromo, who became head coach in 1967.

Then one day at a Louisville Colonels baseball game, Hickman ran into Dromo and the two ended up sitting together. Neither said much until along about the seventh inning. Then Hickman nudged him and said, "Well, John, if you won't referee my games, how about becoming my assistant coach?" Hickman offered Dromo $4,600 a year to serve as assistant football and basketball coach beginning with the 1948-49 season.

From that time until Hickman's retirement 19 years later, Dromo was Hickman's only assistant coach.

"Whenever a coaching job came open, especially in the Southeastern Conference, Adolph Rupp would recommend me," said Dromo. "He wanted me out of the state because we were recruiting some of the kids he wanted." Dromo's duties at U of L included coaching the freshman team, and in 17 seasons his frosh won 233 of 258 games. But his primary job was recruiting. As golf coach, he often played with prospective players. He also took them to baseball games, ate meals in their homes, and became known as the smoothest-talking, best-dressed basketball coach in America.

Fred Holden

As Hickman's assistant, Dromo recruited the first blacks to ever play at U of L — Wade Houston, Sam Smith, and Eddie Whitehead in 1962-63 and Dave Gilbert in 1963-64. Gilbert has fond memories of the sensitivity and understanding Dromo exhibited in that touchy situation.

Gilbert was the only black on the freshman squad, but Dromo made him team captain, which stunned the newcomer.

"You have to remember the times," said Gilbert, now a corporate executive. "The civil-rights movement was just gaining strength in the South. It's hard for me to tell you how much that meant to me, but it's something I've never forgotten."

THE 1967-68 SEASON Hickman didn't leave the cupboard bare. Of the previous season's starters, only Dave Gilbert had graduated. Returnees were Wes Unseld and Fred Holden, both seniors, and juniors Butch Beard and Jerry King. With all this experience, it is no wonder that the Cardinals began the year ranked No. 4 in both major polls.

The Dromo era got under way as most expected it would: with the Cards crushing Georgetown College, 118-86, at Freedom Hall. The game was highlighted by Unseld's record-breaking 45 points. He also grabbed 29 rebounds.

U of L now had to turn its attention to No. 3 Kansas. The game was in Lawrence, and to make matters worse, the Cards were without Holden, who suffered strained ligaments in his knee against Georgetown. But with Unseld and Beard taking charge, Louisville stunned the Jayhawks, 57-51, before 17,000. "We threw a 1-3-1 zone at them, and they didn't know what to do," Dromo said.

As sharp as Louisville had been against Kansas, the reverse was true in the next game, which was against Northwestern. The Cardinals lost, 88-83, despite Unseld's 36 points and 15 rebounds.

After losing at Dayton and winning at Saint Louis, Louisville returned home for a rematch with Kansas. And this time the Jayhawks returned the favor, winning

Butch Beard shoots one of his patented jump shots.

84-76 in two overtimes. Beard scored 24 and Unseld 23, but the team committed 27 turnovers. This left the Cards 3-3 as they headed to New York to participate in the eight-team Holiday Festival.

Marv Selvy, a sophomore from Corbin, Ky., surprised LaSalle in Louisville's first-round win with 19 points. But the Cards got a surprise of their own in the second round when they were upset by Columbia. From there, however, they reeled off four consecutive victories, starting with a Holiday Festival consolation win over Bob Cousy's Boston College team, before losing back-to-back MVC games at Bradley and Cincinnati.

This left the preseason No. 4 team with only an 8-6 record. On January 23, Louisville returned to Freedom Hall to open a five-game homestand. That night it turned back Dayton, 73-72, to avenge a 16-point loss. This was the first of 12 consecutive victories that would send U of L to the NCAA as MVC champion with an overall record of 20-6.

On March 4, Unseld played for the last time as a Louisville Cardinal at Freedom Hall against city foe Bellarmine College. He delighted the crowd with 20 points, and the Cards won, 107-58.

But U of L's first opponent in the NCAA was undefeated Houston (29-0), the nation's No. 1 team because of its victory over UCLA in a historic nationally televised game. For a few fleeting moments, it appeared the Cardinals were primed for an upset. They were leading 13-11 when all that changed.

With Elvin Hayes and teammate Don Chaney in full control, the Cougars outscored Louisville 26-4 in the next few minutes to open a 37-17 lead. When it was over, the Cougars had won, 91-75. The Cards did end their season on a winning note by mauling Kansas State, 93-63, in the third-place game.

THE 1968-69 SEASON It was during this season that the term "Cardiac Cards" was coined. Dromo's team was involved in 11 games decided by four points or fewer.

After reeling off five routine victories to launch the season, Louisville struggled to back-to-back one-point home wins over Florida State and Memphis State. After the 79-78 thriller over Florida State, Dromo told his team

Jerry King takes a shot during a 1970 victory over Bellarmine.

to please refrain from those close calls. "My heart just can't take it," he said.

Despite going 20-4, Louisville fared no better than a tie with Drake for the Missouri Valley Conference title and its automatic NCAA berth. A one-game playoff was scheduled at Wichita on March 10. The winner would go to the NCAA, the loser to the NIT.

Louisville and Drake had played twice during the season, each team winning decisively at home. The playoff, however, proved to be another one of those nailbiters. After trailing most of the way, the Cards pulled within 75-73 in the final minute but Drake hung on to win, 77-73.

While Drake became the darling of the NCAA by reaching the Final Four, extending powerful UCLA, and upending North Carolina for third place, Louisville had to settle for the NIT. The Cards defeated Fordham, 73-70, with Mike Grosso scoring 23 points and corralling 22 rebounds. But Boston College brought the curtain down in the second round, 88-83.

During Beard and King's three varsity years, Louisville had amassed an incredible home record of 39 wins in 40 games, losing only to Kansas in double overtime. Beard had scored 1,580 career points.

THE 1969-70 SEASON Center Mike Grosso would be surrounded by the most talented group of sophomores ever to wear the red and black: Jim Price, Henry Bacon, 6-9 Al Vilcheck, 6-5 Mike Lawhon, and 6-0 Larry Carter. Bacon, Lawhon, and Carter were Louisville natives.

Because of the "Super Sophs," U of L was ranked 17th by *Sports Illustrated*. Still, Dromo knew that only Grosso had bona fide varsity experience when the season opened with Cal-Riverside on December 6.

Even though Louisville won that game, 99-63, Riverside coach Fred Goss sounded a warning when he called the Cardinals disappointing. "Remember, we only have two scholarship players," Goss cautioned. Three nights later, U of L lost by 16 at home to Dayton. It was going to be an interesting year.

By February 18, U of L stood 16-4 and 10-1 in the MVC. Three nights later, Louisville hosted Cincinnati before a Freedom Hall crowd of 15,500, and the Bearcats won a 53-52 squeaker on a pair of free throws by Don Ogeltree.

U of L never recovered, losing three of its last five regular season games for an 18-8 record. On March 15, the Cards were ousted from the NIT by Oklahoma, 74-73, with Garfield Heard scoring 34 for the Sooners.

"We beat ourselves," Dromo said afterward. "Just like we did many other times this year."

CARDINALS QUIZ

12. Although U of L has enjoyed moderate success against teams from the Big Ten, there are two schools from that conference that the Cardinals have never defeated. What teams are they?

THE 1970-71 SEASON Even with the departure of Grosso, Dromo was full of optimism as another season dawned. His super sophs of the previous season were now super juniors. The Cardinals opened with a hard-earned 82-74 victory at Vanderbilt with Vilcheck scoring 31 and getting 13 rebounds against the Commodores' 7-3 center, Steve Turner.

But after returning to the hotel room, Betty Dromo informed team physician Rudy Ellis that her husband wasn't feeling well. "I hadn't been feeling well all day, and my heart was beating so fast," Dromo said later. "I thought it was due to the excitement of the game."

Butch Beard of Louisville drives through the Tampa team for a layup.

At around 1 a.m., the 54-year-old Dromo was transported to St. Francis Hospital in Tulsa, where it was discovered that he had suffered a major heart attack. His coaching career was over.

The team returned to Louisville the following day, and Hickman announced that assistant coach and former player Howard Stacey would assume command for the remainder of the season. Second-year assistant Bill Olsen would continue coaching the freshmen and would serve as Stacey's only aide.

"We'll stay focused and concentrate on winning," Stacey told reporters. "That's what Coach Dromo would want us to do."

Certainly, Stacey's brief coaching stint got off to a brilliant start as Louisville mopped up Georgetown, 115-76, on January 4 and won easily at North Texas later that week. But except for a six-game winning streak, the Cardinals were up and down. Louisville, Saint Louis, and Drake wound up tied for first in the MVC, necessitating a

Al Vilcheck (30) keeps the ball away from a Saint Louis player. This game, which Louisville won 90-76, was played in 1971 at Freedom Hall when Howard Stacey was interim coach.

playoff. The site was Peoria, Ill., with Louisville and Saint Louis vying for the right to play Drake for the NCAA berth. Although the Cards led the Billikens by 19 at one point, it took three free throws by Price to preserve a 68-66 victory. In the finale with Drake, however, nothing went right and the Cardinals lost, 86-71.

For the third consecutive year, Louisville went to the NIT, where it lost to Providence, 64-58. At the conclusion of the season, Dromo met with his players and told them: "I can't coach anymore."

Meanwhile, Stacey accepted the head coaching position at Drake.

A search began to find another coach, and for the first time since World War II, it would be someone with no previous U of L connections.

"You know, when God calls me home, I don't want him to ask me what I did with my life after I stopped coaching," Dromo once said. "I hope He will say, 'John, you were really a good guy.' "

Dromo died September 29, 1992, of a heart attack.

A Burning Desire

Denny Crum (above and below, seated second from left) was an assistant coach on three of UCLA's national championship teams. Crum's last year at UCLA was in 1970-71, the year the Bruins won their seventh NCAA crown and fifth in a row.

Denny Crum had a burning desire to be the head coach at UCLA, where he had played and served as an assistant under John Wooden.

But that was before he found a home in the Bluegrass. More than a quarter-century later, Crum — a native of the San Fernando Valley — has long since dismissed any notion of returning to Los Angeles, even though he still has strong ties there. The 1996-97 season marked his 26th at the University of Louisville.

Early on, though, Crum had no intention of staying for very long at U of L, where his achievements have already earned him a spot in the Naismith Memorial Basketball Hall of Fame (one of only three active college coaches in the Hall.)

"I wanted to go to a school and prove I could be a major-college coach," said Crum, who succeeded John Dromo in 1971. "I figured that when Coach Wooden retired I might have the chance to go back to UCLA as head coach, which was the job I always wanted."

"At the time he left, I thought he'd be the one to succeed me because I knew he was going to do well and he liked the area," Wooden said. "But later, after he became settled in and appreciated, there was no doubt in my mind that he'd never come back."

When Wooden retired in 1975, UCLA Athletic Director J.D. Morgan felt he couldn't match Crum's salary at Louisville — which already exceeded Wooden's $32,000

— and hired Gene Bartow. Crum's most serious flirtation with the Bruins — and the closest he ever came to leaving U of L — came two years later, when Bartow resigned.

When Crum returned to Louisville following an interview with Morgan in 1977, he thought he had coached his last game with the Cardinals.

"I really thought I was going to UCLA," Crum said. "But the day after I got back here, I played golf with some friends and I thought, 'Why would I want to go out there and fight all that traffic and smog and stuff when I have everything here?'

"I had grown to love Louisville, and once you get comfortable with a place and a lifestyle that fits you, it's hard to leave. It's a great place to be a basketball coach or player and a wonderful place to live."

THE BEGINNING Although Crum's only previous head coaching job had been at Pierce Junior College in California, he came to Louisville with the highest letter of recommendation on the planet — that of John Wooden.

After playing two years at Pierce, Crum had transferred to UCLA, where he became an immediate impact player for Wooden. But it wasn't Crum's play that impressed the Wizard of Westwood most. "I could tell early on that here was a kid who was born to coach," Wooden later said. "I never said that about any other player, but I knew right off that Denny had the makings of one day becoming an outstanding coach."

After his graduation from UCLA in 1961, Crum was retained by Wooden as a graduate assistant. "He was bright, alert, and so focused and enthusiastic. But in the early going he was much too critical," Wooden said. "Of course, I knew that was due to immaturity. But players would come to me and say, 'Coach, get that kid off our backs. He's driving us crazy.' I'd say, 'Well, he has to learn. Just remember that it's your best interest he has at heart.' "

In 1961 Crum returned to Pierce as an assistant coach and in 1964 assumed the head position. Wooden continued to follow his career. "Denny had done such a great job that I decided that as soon as we had a vacancy on the staff I'd bring him back." In 1968 that vacancy materialized and Crum returned in the second year of the greatest dynasty college basketball has ever seen. From 1967 to 1973, the Bruins won seven consecutive national championships.

Under Wooden, Crum was the lead recruiter. He brought in players such as Bill Walton, Pete Trgovich, and Keith (later Jamal) Wilkes. By the 1971 season, Wooden knew Crum was ready to assume a head position and did not hesitate in recommending him to Louisville Athletic Director Peck Hickman.

CARDINALS QUIZ

13. *Three schools from the Big Ten have never defeated U of L. What teams are they?*

Denny Crum (center front) and his coaching staff. Surrounding Crum are, left to right, Jerry Jones, Dana Kirk, and Bill Olsen.

Dana Kirk

Crum was in Houston in March 1971, helping prepare the Bruins for yet another national championship, when the call that would change his life came from Louisville. "The call was from Frank Cushing, a good friend of mine who was on the faculty at U of L, and he said they had been inquiring about me," Crum remembered.

"The first time I saw him he had these long sideburns and was wearing a leisure suit," Hickman said in recalling his first impression of Crum. "But then we interviewed him and he blew us all away." About a week after the Bruins beat Villanova to win the NCAA Tournament, Crum, who had also been approached by Virginia Tech, received the call from Hickman offering him the job.

"I took the job at Louisville primarily on the basis of their great basketball tradition," Crum said. "They had a great place to play in Freedom Hall and I thought it was located in an area that would be 360 degrees around as a great recruiting base." As his top assistants, Crum retained former U of L player Bill Olsen to coach the freshmen, and as his top varsity assistant he decided on 35-year-old Dana Kirk, who had coached at Tampa University before officials at that institution decided to discontinue its basketball program.

THE 1971-72 SEASON (FINAL FOUR)

"If I heard it once, I heard it 10 or 15 times," Crum said of that first year. "Everyone said I'd have a pretty good team if I could control Jim Price. I think there were eight or nine seniors on that team, and I can honestly say that I didn't have a single problem with any of them."

Price, a 6-3 senior from Indianapolis, was the main man, considered one of the best guards the Ville had ever produced.

Backing up Price were home-grown Louisvillians Henry Bacon, 6-5 Mike Lawhon, and 6-6 Ron Thomas. The center would be 6-9 Al Vilcheck and first off the bench would be guard Larry Carter, another Louisvillian who had averaged 14 points a game as a starter the previous season.

Louisville opened the season at Florida. "I told them almost daily for the first two weeks prior to our opening game that if they played like they were practicing that we

A young Denny Crum voices his frustration over an official's call.

would lose down there, and that's exactly what happened," Crum said. Florida won by a point, and after that the players began listening to their new coach more closely.

Next came Crum's first victory, a 116-58 laugher over Bellarmine College before 7,149 at Freedom Hall. This was followed by 14 more, including a win over Kansas and a 103-81 victory over Syracuse in the title game of the Holiday Festival in New York City.

The streak came to a screeching halt before Louisville's largest crowd of the year at Freedom Hall on February 2 with Memphis State being the party crasher, 77-69. But the Cards reeled off seven more in a row to run their record to 22-2 before heading to Memphis for a rematch. This time the Tigers won by an even larger margin, 80-65.

At the end of regular-season play, Louisville and Memphis State were tied for the lead in the Missouri Valley Conference. There was only one NCAA tourney berth available for the MVC champion in 1972, so a playoff game was set at Vanderbilt University in Nashville on March 11.

"That was the most electric game I've ever been

Crum poses with his former boss, UCLA's John Wooden.

involved with, maybe up to the Kentucky game in 1983," Crum recalled. "People from both schools were yelling and screaming at each other two hours before tipoff. We were down in the basement in the locker room and could hear them from way down there. It was a war." Louisville won 83-72 to qualify for the NCAA.

Louisville turned back a surprisingly stubborn team from Southwestern Louisiana, 88-84, and then took out Kansas State, 72-65, to win the Midwest Regional. For the first time since 1959 and only the second time ever, Louisville was going to the Final Four.

This left Crum in the awkward yet pleasant position of coaching against his former boss, John Wooden, and

Henry Bacon attempts to block a shot by a Cincinnati player during a game at Freedom Hall. Other U of L players pictured are Jim Price (15) and Al Vilcheck (30).

Jim Price (15) takes a shot against Dayton.

players he had recruited for UCLA. Not only did Louisville have to go up against an undefeated team seeking its sixth straight NCAA crown, but the game was in Los Angeles. UCLA, with the 6-11 Bill Walton dominating the boards, won, 96-77. Two nights later, the Cardinals dropped the third-place game to North Carolina to finish 26-5.

"All the kids worked hard that year and did what they were supposed to do," Crum said. "Once they understood the concept of what we were trying to do, they just kept getting better." Those 26 victories equaled the number amassed by the 1955-56 team that won the NIT and at the time was surpassed only by the 29-6 mark established in 1947-48. Not bad for a rookie coach.

THE 1972-73 SEASON The entire starting lineup from 1971-72 (Price, Thomas, Lawhon, Bacon, and Vilcheck) was gone, but on hand were a couple of multi-talented

6-5 sophomores, Allen Murphy and Junior Bridgeman, who proved to be the nucleus of a team that would win 23 of 30 games and reach the second round of the NIT. Other key players would be 6-9 junior Bill Bunton, guard Terry Howard, and Bill Butler, a tiny forward at 6-2.

This team finished 23-7 overall.

THE 1973-74 SEASON With the top five scorers returning, expectations were naturally high. But a season-opening loss at home to Cincinnati may have been an indication that this would not be a memorable season even though the team finished 21-7 and won the MVC with an 11-1 record.

Murphy and Bridgeman were again the leading scorers with 16.6 and 16.4 scoring averages, respectively. Missing, however, was Bunton, who sat out the year with academic woes.

Highlights included a 117-107 victory over Illinois State. The 224 combined points still stand as a record at U of L.

THE NCAA Evangelist Oral Roberts always told his congregations to expect a miracle, but there wasn't one for Louisville. An Oral Roberts team that had been described by *Sports Illustrated* as big, talented, and without sin upset the Cardinals, 96-93, in the Midwest Regional in Tulsa. A loss to Eddie Sutton's Creighton team in the consolation game brought a dismal end to what was otherwise a very good year.

THE 1974-75 SEASON (FINAL FOUR)

CARDINALS QUIZ

This was the year of Kentuckiana. The Big Three (Indiana, Kentucky, and Louisville) reigned supreme. But in the end, the UCLA dynasty, terminated by North Carolina State in 1974, would return for an encore.

Sports Illustrated went so far as to pick the Cards No. 1 in the nation. Crum knew he held a trump with the return of Murphy, the 1973 MVC Most Valuable Player, and Bridgeman, who had won the same honor in 1973-74. Adding to Crum's high optimism would be the restored eligibility of the 6-9 Bunton and the return of guard Phil Bond, sidelined for health reasons the previous season.

"Murphy wasn't really all that good at creating his own shots, but he was excellent coming off screens and shooting the jumper," recalled assistant coach Jerry Jones. "The way we worked it, most times Murphy would play forward and Bridgeman guard on offense. On defense we would flip-flop them because Junior was a better ball handler and had a little more range on his shot."

14. Louisville has played every Southeastern Conference school at least once, with one exception. Which SEC team has never faced the Cards in basketball?

15. Each year,
U of L's basketball
teams are among the
leaders in home
attendance. The
record for the largest
crowd at a U of L
game in Freedom
Hall is 20,076.
When was that game
played and who was
the opponent?

16. What is the
largest crowd that
U of L has ever
played before?

For reserves, Crum could go to 6-11 freshman Ricky Gallon, the multi-talented Rick Wilson, and free-throw specialist Terry Howard.

Louisville bolted out of the gate with successive wins at Houston, Dayton, and Florida State and finished December at 7-0. Yet there were signs of discontent among some of the younger players, who felt they weren't getting enough playing time.

On January 11, the Cardinals were 10-0 when they landed in Las Cruces for a game with New Mexico State. The grumbling from the reserves had become so intense that Bridgeman called for a meeting of the players. During the lengthy session some said they felt the starters weren't putting out 100 percent and were afraid to be taken out of a game. "You should have enough confidence in us to let us come in and give you a break," one reserve contended.

The starters agreed and the meeting concluded on a positive note. Bridgeman emphasized to each player that no one, not even the coaches, was to know about the meeting. However, when Howard placed a call to his wife in Louisville, the first thing she asked was how the meeting went.

"How did you know about it?" Howard asked. She said it had been on television. It turned out that a cameraman had heard that there was going to be a secret meeting and telephoned the news back to his station.

Louisville ran its streak to 13-0 before being derailed January 25 at Bradley, a team it had beaten in overtime in Louisville. The only other regular-season loss was at Tulsa on February 8. But there were several scares.

The regular-season game fans most remember occurred at home on February 16 against a Saint Louis team that U of L was expected to squash. The strategy of the badly outmanned Billikens was to hold the ball, lull the defenders to sleep, and slip in for the easy basket. The plan was working so well that by halftime Saint Louis led, 41-26. Many of the shocked fans booed the Cardinals as they left the floor.

Early in the second half, things went from bad to worse. At one point, Crum benched all of his starters. But nothing helped. With 13:23 to go, Saint Louis led 59-36. In desperation, he called a time-out, and assistant coach Bill Olsen came up with a plan. "Look, fellas, this is getting out of hand," Olsen said. "Why don't we just forget everything we've practiced this week and play like it's a pickup game in Shawnee Park." Crum agreed it was worth a try.

Within two minutes, the crowd was screaming. Years later, Saint Louis player Carl Johnson discussed with a U of L player Louisville's 75-68 triumph that night: "You know, when we went into that game, we didn't think we had a shot. But by the time we figured we were gonna pull off the upset, Crum called a time-out. Then all hell broke loose. I never did know what happened during that time-out."

After finishing 24-2 and winning the MVC in its last year as a member, Louisville was assigned to the Midwest Regional's preliminary round in Tulsa. After rallying to beat Rutgers, 91-78, the Cards advanced again to Las Cruces and dispatched Cincinnati's 16-game winning streak before taking on Maryland, which billed itself "The UCLA of the East," for the right to advance to San Diego, site of the Final Four. Maryland, which had disposed of Notre Dame and Adrian Dantley with surprising ease, trailed by only four with four minutes left. But led by tourney MVP Phil Bond, Louisville pulled away to win, 96-82.

"In the last few minutes of the game we could sense that their confidence was diminishing," said Bond. "And it was then that we put them away."

Now it was on to San Diego, where the old professor, John Wooden, awaited with yet another powerful UCLA team. But this time, Crum knew he had the horses to win — even against the master.

Junior Bridgeman cuts down the nets in Las Cruces following Louisville's win over Maryland in the NCAA Midwest Regional final.

Going into the NCAA Tournament, there was no doubt that undefeated Indiana was the team to beat. But suddenly the Hoosiers were gone, ousted by a massive Kentucky team they had beaten by 24 in December. For the only time in history, both UK and U of L were in the Final Four, and they could meet in the national championship.

All week, Crum and Kentucky's Joe Hall tried to shelter their players from all the Dream Game hype. Then a comment by Crum was aired in which he said he would not trade his players for anyone on Kentucky's team.

"Some people took it out of context because they thought I meant that our kids were better than Kentucky's. But my point was that our kids were better suited for our system, just as Kentucky's were for the type of game they played," he explained later. "Some fans got bent out of shape and thought I was being brash and arrogant. I wasn't demeaning their system at all. We did feel that we could beat Kentucky because we felt we were a lot quicker, but certainly they were an outstanding team to have beaten Indiana."

"We were plenty worried about Louisville," recalled UCLA's David Meyers. "We had seen their films and when you compared them to us they looked like another UCLA. We saw in the films that those guys played above the rim just like we did and they were quick, just like we were. We knew they were really going to be tough."

In addition to Meyers, an All-American, the Bruins had Richard Washington, Pete Trgovich, Marques Johnson, and Andre McCarter. Phil Bond had first-hand knowledge of McCarter, whom he would be guarding.

"In high school I had a friend who knew all there was to know about basketball, and one day we were playing one-on-one," Bond recalled. "I said I was Dr. J and he said he was some guy I never heard of named Andre McCarter. Then my friend said McCarter was a high school sensation from Philadelphia and that someday he would be playing on a national championship team."

Louisville took an early nine-point lead but UCLA cut it to 37-33 at halftime with a rally that included three straight baskets by Trgovich. With five minutes left in the game, the Cards still had a four-point lead, and for a fleeting instant, Bond thought, "It seemed just like Maryland." But Johnson's tip-in with 37 seconds to go brought the Bruins even at 65-65. Louisville had one final chance in regulation, but a shot from the corner by Bridgeman caromed off the rim.

Since assuming the U of L post in 1971, Crum's teams had been forced into overtime five times and won them all. A sixth straight seemed likely when Allen Murphy took charge. He scored Louisville's next seven points,

"People blame Terry (Howard) for the (UCLA) loss, but that's ridiculous. That wasn't the only free throw we didn't hit that day. It just happened to be at the end of the game. We made two or three turnovers down the stretch. A lot of things that could have happened or should have didn't. And we lost. I guess it was like fate taking care of UCLA and Coach Wooden."
— *Denny Crum*

and his basket at 1:17 gave the Cards a 74-71 lead.

But Meyers retaliated with two free throws with 37 seconds remaining. By now reserves were being used by both teams. For Louisville there was Howard, who was a perfect 28-for-28 at the free-throw line for the season. For UCLA there was Jim Spillane.

"If you have to foul, don't foul Howard," Wooden warned during a time-out. "He's perfect from the line." But with 19 seconds to go an overzealous Spillane bumped Howard.

For the only time all season, Howard's free throw rattled around the rim and popped out. Washington grabbed the rebound for the Bruins. After another time-out, they worked the ball around and Johnson hit a 12-footer on the baseline with two seconds left. UCLA had won, 75-74.

Junior Bridgeman has no trouble playing above the rim on this play while UCLA players look on during the 1975 Final Four game at San Diego. Louisville's No. 20 is Allen Murphy.

Louisville's Allen Murphy is surrounded by UCLA players including Richard Washington, who leaps in the air to defend. Washington's shot in overtime eliminated the Cardinals from the 1975 NCAA Final Four.

After the game, Wooden sought out Crum to tell him that this was one of the greatest games he had ever been associated with. "If we had to lose, I'm glad it was to you, Coach," Crum said and each headed to his locker room.

"Suddenly I saw all the flashing lights, and I wasn't feeling very well," Wooden remembered. "When I thought of all the interviews and bright lights associated with championship night, it dawned on me that I didn't want to do this anymore." In the UCLA locker room, the exuberant players became silent, waiting for Wooden to tell them that they had played a great game, had beaten a great team, and now it was time to start thinking about Kentucky. They heard this instead: "I want to say that over the years I've been fortunate enough to have many great teams. But I have never been more proud of any of them than I am of this team, which is the last one I will ever coach." He turned and walked into the hallway, leaving his players and members of the press stunned.

Two nights later he coached the Bruins to a 92-85 win over Kentucky to capture his 10th and last NCAA crown. Louisville took third place with an overtime win over Syracuse to finish 28-3, its best record ever.

THE 1975-76 SEASON Louisville was now a member of the Metro Six Conference, joining archrival Memphis State, Cincinnati, Saint Louis, Georgia Tech, and Tulane. Two months after its inception, the NCAA made an unprecedented move by awarding Metro Six an automatic berth in the NCAA Tournament. The bid would be decided by a postseason tournament at Freedom Hall.

Bridgeman, Murphy, and Bunton were gone, leaving a starting lineup of two juniors (Wesley Cox and Phillip Bond), two sophomores (Ricky Gallon and Rick Wilson) and freshman Larry Williams. Yet the team started strongly, winning seven of eight before a three-game skid early in January.

Darrell Griffith

Then the Cards reeled off 11 straight wins and finished regular-season play at 20-6. Memphis State, however, took them out in the first round of the initial Metro Tournament, 87-76. They had to settle for the NIT.

For the second straight year, the hype was that Louisville and Kentucky were going to play for the first time since 1959. Not for a national championship, as would have been the case in San Diego in 1975, but in the semifinal round of the NIT. But Providence stopped Louisville, 73-67, and Kentucky, the eventual champion, took out Providence in the semifinals.

THE 1976-77 SEASON Whenever Crum talks about his best teams, he always refers to 1976-77 as "the one that got away."

On March 22, 1975, the same day U of L defeated Maryland to reach the Final Four, Darrell Griffith and Bobby Turner led Male, coached by U of L alumnus Wade Houston, to the Kentucky state championship. Two seasons later, all three would take their acts to U of L — Griffith and Turner as players, Houston as an assistant coach.

At a news conference at which he announced that U of L was his choice, Griffith said he had two goals. One was to graduate in four years. The second was to be a member of an NCAA championship team.

Joining him in the starting lineup in 1976-77 were Cox, Wilson, Williams, and Gallon. And for the second consecutive year, all starters would average in double figures.

After escaping with a five-point overtime win at Vanderbilt in the opener, U of L returned home to drop a 76-75 decision to Syracuse. After two home wins, the Cards lost at Purdue, 72-70.

But on December 18, Crum took his team to Milwaukee for a game with Al McGuire's Marquette Warriors and came away with a 78-75 overtime victory against a team that three months later would stun North Carolina to win the national championship.

From there, Louisville reeled off 14 more wins before being stopped at Nevada Las Vegas 99-96 on February 12. "I thought we were really playing well and would be a definite factor in the NCAA," Crum remarked. But in the

This slam by Darrell Griffith in a game against Georgia Tech is one reason the Louisville squads of his era were known as the "Doctors of Dunk." This game was during Griffith's sophomore season.

next game, at Tulsa, Williams sustained a broken foot.

"We just didn't have anybody to take Larry's place, and it was like the air went out of the ball," Crum said. The Cards lost two of their last four regular-season games, then were beaten by Georgia Tech in the Metro Tournament.

THE 1977-78 SEASON A season-opening loss at Providence was followed by seven straight victories before Georgia managed a 73-70 upset win in the title game of the Louisville Holiday Classic. From there, led by Griffith and Wilson, the Cards reeled off nine of the next 10 for a 16-3 mark. Then the team hit the skids, losing in succession at Georgia Tech, Florida State, and Minnesota before capping the regular season with three straight victories.

In the Metro Conference Tournament at Cincinnati, U of L easily ousted Tulane, 93-64, then outlasted Memphis, 67-62, and Florida State, 94-93, to earn the league's NCAA bid.

Louisville was sent to Tulsa for a preliminary game in the Midwest Regional and defeated St. John's, 76-68. From there, the Cards advanced to Lawrence, Kan., but dropped a heartbreaking 90-89 double-overtime decision to DePaul.

THE 1978-79 SEASON Replacing the 6-10 Ricky Gallon in the middle would be one of Crum's major concerns. And he would also have to plug a hole vacated by Rick Wilson. The most notable newcomers would be 6-8 Scooter McCray of Mt. Vernon, N.Y., guard Jerry Eaves of Louisville's Ballard High School, and a pair of Georgia All-Staters, Derek Smith and Wiley Brown.

CARDINALS QUIZ

17. Western Kentucky and San Francisco were the opponents when Freedom Hall was dedicated in 1956. However, this was not the first official game played in the facility. What teams played in that first game, which took place December 22, 1956?

Louisville Coach Denny Crum voices his opinion to an official.

Darrell Griffith often stood head and shoulders above all opponents, just as he does on this play.

The Cards entered their holiday tournament with a 7-2 record. But after beating Wisconsin, they again lost the championship game to a Southeastern Conference team. This time it was Mississippi State. But then Louisville mounted a 13-game winning streak with victims including Memphis State (103-82), Maryland, and — twice apiece — Florida State and Cincinnati.

But on February 10, the team dropped a 71-55 decision at Marquette and never rebounded, losing five of its last eight.

After beating South Alabama, 69-66, the Cardinals moved into the NCAA Midwest Regional semifinals against Eddie Sutton's Arkansas Razorbacks and were promptly eliminated, 73-62. Nothing went right for Griffith in that game, and early in the second half, Crum took him out. After the season critics reminded Griffith that he had only one more year to fulfill his No. 2 goal.

THE 1979-80 SEASON (NCAA CHAMPIONS)

Darrell Griffith knew full well what the critics had been saying. This was the time to put up or shut up.

Louisville's road to Indianapolis actually began in the

On the morning of the 1980 championship game, Wiley Brown barely avoided a catastrophe. Early in his life, Brown had been involved in a freak accident, and one of his thumbs had to be amputated. In order to help him grip the ball, Louisville's team physician Rudy Ellis and trainer Jerry May devised a hollow, plastic thumb that was fitted over Brown's stub. Brown had placed the thumb on a table at breakfast in a restaurant and forgot it. The next hour was spent frantically searching through the dumpster until the thumb was found.

summer of 1979 when Griffith began spending most of his nights alone in Crawford Gym, dribbling around chairs, shooting over a volleyball net, and playing against imaginary opponents. Hour after hour after hour. "This was my senior year and I was determined to make good," he would later say. "I not only wanted to improve, but I knew I had to stay focused."

In spite of Griffith's dedication, the Cardinals were hardly the team to beat going into the season. They appeared to be too young.

"In addition to Griff's leadership, one thing we did have that year is depth," Crum noted. Derek Smith, Wiley Brown, Scooter McCray, and Jerry Eaves were only sophomores. Roger Burkman was a junior and Rodney McCray, Scooter's brother, was but a freshman.

LEADER BY EXAMPLE "In the first few days of practice, everyone was hyped up and excited but as time wore on, the energy seemed to die down. But it didn't die down for me," Griffith said. "I maintained that pace day in and day out, never letting up. Some of the guys thought I was showing off, but I really wasn't. I was trying to lead by example."

Gradually the feeling became contagious, and soon every day at practice became a war. Crum couldn't have been happier.

After a hard-fought two-point win over South Alabama in the opener, the Cardinals easily wiped up Tennessee-Chattanooga before heading to Knoxville for a game with Tennessee on December 8. There they lost starting center Scooter McCray to a knee injury for the remainder of the season. He was replaced by his younger brother.

Until then, Rodney had accepted the fact that he would only be a reserve in his first year. In practice he didn't spend a lot of extra time running up and down the floor. He did only what he was asked. Now all of that changed.

"When Rodney first came out, I never saw anybody with more baby fat," Burkman related. "He wouldn't do anything extra in practice. But after Scooter went down, he became totally dedicated. By the end of the year, he could take the ball in midair and hit you on a dime. And that baby fat had disappeared."

On December 19, second-ranked Ohio State invaded Freedom Hall and a crowd that exceeded 16,000 came away convinced that this could indeed be a dynamite year. The Cards ripped the Buckeyes by 10 to go 6-0.

This win vaulted Louisville into The Associated Press top five, where it would remain for most of the season. But on the way to Honolulu, where the Cards were to participate in the eight-team Rainbow Classic, they stopped in Provo to take on Utah. A stunning last-second

Griff finds opposition from a St. John's player during a 1980 game at Madison Square Garden. Louisville won, 76-71.

shot sent them reeling to their first loss of the year, 71-69.

After beating Princeton in its Rainbow Classic opener, Louisville was paired with Illinois. The Cards took an early lead against the Illini but the good times ended when Lou Henson called for a 1-2-2 zone. "We pack everybody inside and give them the outside shot," Henson said. For Louisville's outside shooters, it became miss, miss, miss, and miss some more.

"I don't think we ever played against a team that just lets you shoot like this," assistant Jerry Jones remarked to Crum at one point. Illinois won, 77-64.

The next night, Louisville picked up the third-place trophy by topping Nebraska. It was the first of 18 consecutive wins.

In this stretch Griffith was often phenomenal. He scored 35 against West Virginia, 31 against Memphis State, and 28 at Saint Louis. But in case of a rare off night, his supporting cast was always there.

Louisville, 25-2, now had only two remaining games. The first would be at Madison Square Garden against Iona and the finale at Florida State.

Against Iona, before a capacity Garden crowd of 18,592, Louisville was going to "strut its stuff," as one coach put it. "Boy, we were really gonna show 'em."

"Iona wasn't a big-name team, but they had a big guy everybody respected named Jeff Ruland," Crum recalled. "Kentucky had recruited him very heavily. And their coach was a fiery young man named Jim Valvano. Unfortunately, our guys seemed more interested in sightseeing than concentrating on basketball. This was homecoming for Rodney and Scooter, and they were intent on showing the others a good time."

Iona won, 77-60. When the Cards returned to Louisville, Griffith called another meeting. "Guys, we got embarrassed up there in New York," he told his teammates. "We gotta get our act together fast, or it's gonna be all over for us."

Wiley Brown (41) and Rodney McCray vie for a rebound during the 1980 NCAA title game with UCLA.

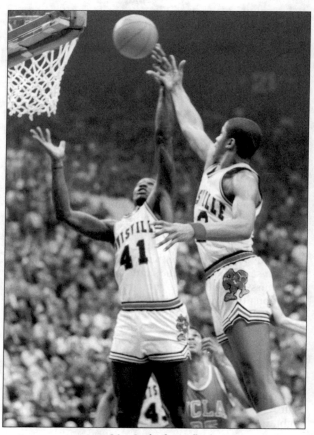

When the team landed at the airport in Tallahassee for the finale with Florida State, Crum entered the terminal and spotted a dime on the floor. "I remembered that whenever Coach Wooden would find a penny he'd pick it up and put it in the instep of his left shoe. Then he'd say, 'Well, that's one more victory.' I figured that dime would be enough to carry us the rest of the way, so I placed it in the instep of my left shoe."

After beating Florida State, Louisville returned to Freedom Hall for the Metro Conference Tournament. As regular-season champions, the Cards received a first-round bye. Then they polished off Memphis State, 84-65, and Florida State, 81-72, to clinch the automatic NCAA berth.

Louisville was seeded No. 2 in the Midwest Regional behind Louisiana State, which was led by Louisvillian Rudy Macklin and DeWayne Scales. The first stop was Lincoln, Neb., and the opponent was Kansas State, a team the Cardinals had beaten by 12 at Freedom Hall in January. For most of the night it appeared that this might be the end of the line for Griffith and Company.

"That was a scary game for us," Griffith said. "I was really worried because I fouled out and when we went to overtime I knew it was out of my hands. I could only watch and pray, and I remember thinking that this might be the last time I ever wear a U of L uniform."

As the final seconds ticked down in overtime, Louisville had possession with the score 69-69. Crum called a time-out and set up a play. Although it wasn't exactly the play Crum had drawn, reserve guard Tony Branch threw up what appeared to be a totally illogical, off-balance shot. The ball neatly slipped through the net and Louisville won.

That victory advanced Louisville to The Summit in Houston along with LSU, Missouri, and Texas A & M. The Aggies would be the Cardinals' second-round foe. Again the game went into overtime, but this time the outcome was decided early in the extra period. U of L won, 66-55.

During the closing seconds, with the outcome no longer in doubt, Branch was fouled. It suddenly dawned on Crum that his top reserve had not missed a free throw the entire season. Remembering what had happened to Terry Howard in 1975, he instructed Branch to intentionally miss.

LSU, Louisville's next opponent, was the leading field-goal shooting team in the nation, the Southeastern Conference champion, and twice conqueror of No. 1 Mideast seed Kentucky.

In the early going, it was a game of streaks. First, Louisville jumped out 21-13. Then LSU went on a 16-0 run. Finally, the Cards closed the half with a 10-0 spurt to lead, 31-29. Early in the second half, Griffith was

CARDINALS QUIZ

18. When was Louisville's first game at Freedom Hall and what school was the opponent?

CARDINALS QUIZ

19. Only two freshmen have ever been voted Most Valuable Player of an NCAA Tournament Final Four. One attended U of L. Who was he?

taken out because of foul trouble. Smith and Brown put the clamps on Macklin, and Louisville's ever-present full-court press began paying off. Quickly, the Tigers fell from contention and Louisville went on to win, 86-66.

For the third time, Crum was taking a team to the Final Four. The site would be 120 miles up Interstate 65 at Market Square Arena in Indianapolis.

Out of the East Regional came Iowa, which had finished only fourth in the Big Ten. From the Mideast came Purdue, another Big Ten entry, having placed third in that league. Led by Joe Barry Carroll, the Boilermakers gave the Hoosier State a representative in its first Final Four party. From the West came UCLA, which had ousted top-ranked DePaul and Big Ten champion Ohio State. UCLA was a young team, and there was a new guy in charge in North Carolina product Larry Brown. The Bruins at one point had been 8-6. Now they were 21-9.

The Cardinals were paired against Iowa in the opener on Saturday, March 22. Louisville took control early, and Griffith was never more effective. From the tipoff, it became apparent that this would be a war between Griff and Ronnie Lester, who had been heavily recruited by U of L. But a few minutes into the game, Lester went down with a badly injured knee following a

Louisville All-American Darrell Griffith receives an award from U of L Athletic Director Bud Olsen during the Cardinals' 1995 game with Temple's Owls. The 1980 team was honored 15 years after winning the national championship.

collision with Burkman.

With Lester on the sidelines and Griffith on a rampage, there was no question that for the first time, the Cardinals would be advancing to the championship. Griffith finished the 80-72 victory with 34 points, then started looking ahead to UCLA, which had defeated Purdue.

REMEMBERING A DYING FRIEND In a pregame interview before a nationwide television audience, Griffith vowed that Louisville was going to win it for his friend Jerry Stringer, who was dying of bone cancer. Stringer had been Griffith's teammate at Male when the Bulldogs won the state championship in 1975. He and his twin brother, James, had come to U of L as non-scholarship players. "Jerry was such a likeable kid that I kept him on our JV team here," assistant coach Jerry Jones said.

U of L and UCLA appeared nervous in the early going, and neither could gain more than a four-point advantage. Griffith's 20-foot jump shot in the final seconds left UCLA in front, 28-26, at the break.

"Denny really chewed our butts at halftime and even called us quitters, and I thought, 'Wait a minute. He's stepping on our toes,' " Derek Smith said.

In the second half, successive lay-ups by Eaves, Brown, and Griffith brought the Cardinals a 36-32 advantage. UCLA caught up at 38-all. From there, the lead seesawed. A lay-up by Mike Sanders with 6:30 to go allowed UCLA to open its biggest lead of the night at 50-45.

"I knew we still had a chance and wanted to make sure the other guys hadn't lost that look of determination and that the fire in their eyes hadn't gone out," said Griffith. "I could tell it was still there, and we remained totally focused."

Griff countered with a close-in shot, was fouled, and completed the three-point play to quickly slice the deficit to 50-48. But UCLA came right back on a pair of freebies by Sanders. Griffith and Kiki Vandeweghe traded baskets, and UCLA led, 54-50.

Then Vandeweghe came up with a steal and headed for what appeared to be an uncontested lay-up. This, Crum feared, could be the fatal blow. But an alert Eaves ran in front of Vandeweghe, breaking his stride. Vandeweghe lunged for the basket, missed the lay-up, and Brown snared the rebound. A short time later Eaves sank a 17-footer. UCLA's lead, instead of 56-50, was 54-52.

"I could have easily made it," Vandeweghe would later say. "But when the guy ran in front of me, I had to change my stride to avoid a possible charging foul."

At that point, Louisville turned up the pressure and UCLA became erratic. With 3:10 remaining, Rod Foster

CARDINALS QUIZ

20. *Who was the first U of L player selected to an NCAA All-Final Four team?*

CARDINALS QUIZ

21. *Who was the captain of the first Cardinal team that had a winning season — in 1915-16?*

vaulted through Louisville's pressing defenders and put up a bad shot. A pass to Eaves resulted in a tying lay-up at 2:54. Some 30 seconds later, Griffith drilled an 18-footer and Louisville led, 56-54. UCLA would not score again.

When it was over, Louisville had registered the last nine points to win, 59-54. Griffith's No. 2 goal had been achieved. U of L was truly No. 1.

"For some of the guys what we had achieved didn't sink in for awhile," Griffith recalled. "But for me, it hit like a rock at the very moment the game ended and it was wonderful. I was happy for me because I had achieved my goals. And I was happy for my teammates and my coaches. And then there were our fans, who had waited patiently for so long."

"I can remember my feelings at the time," Crum would reflect in later years. "I felt so happy for the kids because they had worked so hard. But for me personally, it was a feeling of relief. 'Crum had finally won the big one,' the media would say, so the monkey was forever off my back. I guess that was the way it was supposed to be because we had lost to UCLA in 1971-72 and 1974-75 in the Final Four. The third time really was a charm for us."

A longtime dream is fulfilled as Darrell Griffith is surrounded by happy fans following Louisville's 59-54 victory over UCLA in the 1980 NCAA championship game at Indianapolis.

Before leaving to meet Governor John Brown in Frankfort and President Jimmy Carter at the White House, Griffith had one more stop to make. He paid a visit to his hospitalized friend, Jerry Stringer, and placed one of the game nets in his hand. "This is for you, brother," Griffith said. Jerry died a short time later.

Griffith went on to star for the Utah Jazz of the NBA.

The 1980 NCAA champions were honored 15 years later, at the 1995 game against Temple. Front row, left to right, are Jerry May, Greg Deuser, Roger Burkman, Denny Crum, Darrell Griffith, Tony Branch and Dr. Rudy Ellis. Back row, Jerry Jones, Daryl Cleveland, Marty Pulliam, Scooter McCray, Wiley Brown, Derek Smith, Wade Houston and Bill Olsen.

Masterful Strokes

THE 1980-81 SEASON Even though the Cardinals lost the most prolific scorer in their history in Darrell Griffith, the four other starters from the NCAA championship team returned. They were Derek Smith, Rodney McCray, Jerry Eaves, and Wiley Brown. And backing them up were Roger Burkman, Poncho Wright, and Scooter McCray, now fully recovered from the knee injury that had kept him sidelined in 1979-80. To boot were a pair of promising freshmen from Mississippi: 6-8 Charles Jones and 6-3 Lancaster Gordon. Little wonder that Louisville followers were calling for a "RE-peat."

Denny Crum

But things began going haywire almost from the opening tip of the opening game against DePaul, led by multi-talented Mark Aguirre and Terry Cummings. This was the annual Tip-Off Classic at Springfield, Mass. The 86-80 loss to Ray Meyer's Blue Demons was the first woe in a dismal 2-7 start.

Things bottomed out in a 64-47 loss at Kansas State in early January. That's when Crum decided to make a lineup change, inserting the two freshmen, Jones at center and Gordon at guard.

"I decided that if we were going to lose, we might as well lose with guys who were going to be here awhile," Crum said. Beginning with a 73-53 win over Tulane, the Cardinals rolled to 19 victories in their next 20 games. They won the Metro Conference with an 11-1 record and then took the Metro Tournament by beating Virginia Tech, 81-68, and slowdown-minded Cincinnati, 42-31.

CARDINALS QUIZ

22. Which U of L player ranks 25th on the NCAA's all-time career list for field-goal percentage?

Louisville was seeded No. 4 in the Midwest Regional at Austin, Texas. First up against the defending champion was Arkansas, the last team to beat the Cardinals in NCAA play.

With three minutes to play, Arkansas led by seven, but the Cards fought back to within 72-71 on a shot by Wright with 35 seconds to go. When an Arkansas pass sailed out of bounds with 13 seconds left, the Cards had a chance. Smith followed Wright's missed shot, and Louisville eased ahead 73-72. Arkansas coach Eddie Sutton called time-out with five seconds remaining, hoping for a miracle. That's exactly what he got, thanks to U.S. Reed. Dribbling until the final instant, Reed let loose with a bomb from 50 feet, getting it off a fraction of a second before the final buzzer. The ball swished. Louisville's reign as champion was over.

At least Reed was honest about his game-winning

shot. "I threw up a prayer," he said. "And to the glory of God, I hit the shot."

THE 1981-82 SEASON (FINAL FOUR)

Three starters from the 1980 NCAA championship team — Derek Smith, Wiley Brown, and Jerry Eaves — were seniors now. And there were three more seniors on the bench: Poncho Wright, Marty Pulliam, and Greg Deuser. Throw into that veteran mix the McCray brothers, sophomores Lancaster Gordon and Charles

Poncho Wright, one of Louisville's premier reserves, is shown here in a game against Western Kentucky.

Members of the Lady Birds' drill team are joined by the Cardinal Bird.

Jones, and freshmen Milt Wagner and Manuel Forrest, and the Cards had a legitimate title contender.

But the road proved much bumpier than expected. During one stretch in January, the Cards dropped four straight, including an absolute drubbing from Ralph Sampson (26 points and 10 rebounds) and Virginia at Freedom Hall.

Then, suddenly it was March and all was right again. They reeled off victories in their last six regular-season games, plus two more in the Metro Conference Tournament. And all feelings of dejection following an 11-point loss to Memphis State in the championship game of the Metro on March 7 were immediately discarded when the NCAA pairings were announced later that same day.

From the moment the Mideast Regional bracket flashed onto television screens, shouts of joy went up throughout the commonwealth. At long last, after 23 years, Kentucky's hardwood giants were going to meet again, this time at Vanderbilt University.

The only catch seemed to be a trivial matter. Kentucky had to get past unheralded Middle Tennessee in Thursday night's opening-round session. The Cards were secure with a bye into the second round.

By Monday afternoon, 24 hours after the seedings had been made public, the souvenir business in Louisville and Lexington was booming. The term "Dream Game" had been coined and was stamped across thousands of shirts, buttons, and bumper stickers. Fans were ready to donate blood or sell body parts in order to obtain tickets to the big show in Nashville.

With Crum hospitalized because of a kidney stone, coaching duties fell to his assistants. "We began that week preparing for both Kentucky and Middle Tennessee, but there was no doubt who our players were thinking about," assistant Jerry Jones said. "Then the other coaches and I went down to Nashville to scout the UK-Middle game and we were surrounded by all the UK-U of L hype. That was all anybody was talking about. This was on Thursday, and our game would be Saturday afternoon."

What happened that night ranks as one of basketball's wonders of the world: Kentucky lost, 50-44. Other than the souvenir vendors and UK diehards, nobody was more disappointed in the outcome than the Louisville players and their lengthy line of followers. "For the first time in my life, I pulled for Kentucky," said Derek Smith. "But it wasn't to be."

Middle Tennessee proved no match for the quicker, taller Cardinals, and Louisville advanced to the round of 16 by winning, 81-56. In the Mideast semifinal round in Birmingham, U of L was joined by Virginia, Minnesota, and host Alabama-Birmingham. First up for the Cards was Minnesota.

Louisville overcame the Gophers and their 7-3 center, Randy Breuer, in a close one, 67-61. But the big news came when UAB stunned top-seeded Virginia, 68-66. With Sampson and the Cavaliers out of the way, the

Assistant Coach Bobby Dotson (center) makes a point with an official while Wade Houston looks on at right during a 1982 game.

A large, happy group of U of L fans greeted the team at Standiford Field in Louisville after the Cards won the 1982 Mideast Regional at Birmingham.

Cards looked forward to taking on Gene Bartow's dangerous Blazers, even though the game was to be played on UAB's home court.

Before a hostile crowd of 16,674, U of L held on to win, 75-68, to advance to the Final Four for the second time in three years. Charles Jones led U of L's balanced scoring attack with 19 points, while Smith, despite receiving six stitches and a dislocated jaw, added 14.

As Wagner put it, Louisville was now prepared to "roam in the Dome" — the Louisiana Superdome. Awaiting the Cards were John Thompson's Georgetown Hoyas and their 7-1 All-American center, Patrick Ewing. The crowd would exceed 61,000, and no U of L team had ever performed to such a multitude. North Carolina, runner-up in 1981, and Houston completed the quartet.

Surprisingly, the Georgetown-Louisville game lacked excitement for the most part. With five minutes left, U of L trimmed a nine-point deficit to 47-42. But the Hoyas hung on to win, 50-46. "We had to struggle for every point we got," Thompson said.

Two nights later, North Carolina won its first title since 1957.

THE 1982-83 SEASON (DREAM GAME & THE FINAL FOUR)

Gone were Smith, Brown, Eaves, and Wright. But an abundance of talent was returning. For starters there was Gordon, who had been the No. 3 scorer as a sophomore. Other returnees were Jones, Wagner, and the McCrays, both now seniors. New faces were Billy Thompson, rated by some as the top prospect in the nation, and Jeff Hall, an All-State player from the Ashland, Ky., area. Other

Kentucky natives included Robbie Valentine of Radcliff and Manuel Forrest of Louisville.

Just as Darrell Griffith had been the team leader in 1979-80, this year's leaders would be the McCray brothers. And what they had to offer was a quiet confidence that quickly spread through the Louisville camp.

Louisville displayed power early by winning the Great Alaska Shootout in Anchorage in late November, putting away Florida, Washington, and Vanderbilt. In the final against the Commodores, Gordon collected 24 points and Wagner 17 in U of L's 80-70 victory.

Following a 28-point victory at Santa Clara, the Cards went flat and lost their home-opener to Purdue on December 4. It would be the team's only Freedom Hall loss the entire season and was followed by home triumphs over Eastern Kentucky, South Alabama, Oklahoma State, and North Carolina State. At the time, the 57-52 victory over Jim Valvano's Wolfpack appeared to carry no significant meaning. Few who were there even considered the possibility that the team Louisville defeated that day would claim the NCAA crown at the end of the season.

A week later, the Cards journeyed to Los Angeles, where for the first time since Crum's arrival in 1971 they would be meeting UCLA in a regular-season game. It also would be the first meeting between the two since the NCAA championship game of 1980. UCLA won, 76-72, to hand Louisville its second defeat.

Louisville countered by reeling off eight victories in a row, including a nationally televised win over DePaul to run its glamorous record to 16-2.

But just as they had done the previous year, the Cardinals ran into a wall when they confronted Virginia, losing 98-81. Virginia shot 64 percent and made 28 of 31 free throws. But on February 2 at Cincinnati, the Cards began constructing a winning streak that would reach 16.

Rodney, above, and Scooter McCray, below, were mainstays at U of L during the early 1980s.

On March 2, 1983, U of L joined an elite group of schools by gaining its 1,000th victory in a 73-64 win at Virginia Tech.

Charles Jones

In its 29th and next-to-last game of the regular season, Louisville defeated Virginia Tech in Blacksburg for the school's 1,000th victory. This left the Cardinals undefeated in Metro Conference play heading into the season finale at Memphis State.

With the teams deadlocked 62-62 in overtime, a Tiger player missed two free throws that might have been decisive. Seconds later Wagner was fouled and went to the line for Louisville. Without breaking a sweat, he sank both shots to provide the winning margin.

Six days later, on March 12 in Cincinnati, Louisville and Memphis State met in the semifinals of the Metro Conference Tournament and Louisville won a little easier — by three points. The Cards then beat Tulane in the final.

This time there was no joy in Louisville when the NCAA pairings were announced, even though for the second straight year U of L and UK were both placed in the Mideast Regional. No one dared whisper about the possibility of a "Dream Game." Louisville's first stop would

Denny Crum

be Roberts Stadium in Evansville, where it would play the winner of a game between Marquette and Tennessee.

The news did not go over well on Belknap Campus. For one thing, one of the Midwest first-round sites was Freedom Hall (in 1983, a team could be assigned to play at its home facility). With this in mind, some 15,000 U of L fans and students had gobbled up tickets for those games, expecting Louisville would play at home. Crum was livid because he felt Louisville's 29-3 record should have been rewarded with a home seed. He also looked upon the Mideast as the toughest regional.

Even after Louisville whipped Tennessee, 70-57, and Kentucky eliminated Ohio University, fans of both schools were at best cautiously optimistic about a showdown in Knoxville, Tenn.

Still, seldom had the Mideast semifinal round drawn such an interesting field. Indiana, Kentucky, Louisville, and Arkansas were the candidates. And, regardless of who played whom, all possible matches were intriguing. For example, what could be a more attractive way for Indiana to reach the Final Four than by beating Kentucky's two giants? What more could UK fans ask for than to arrive in Albuquerque having conquered the teams they resented the most in IU and Louisville? And to the diehard Cardinal fan, what could top beating Arkansas two years after the U.S. Reed fling, then eliminating Indiana? Or, better yet, Kentucky?

The opener paired Kentucky against the Hoosiers. All year, the Kentucky players had been accused of not wanting to play Louisville, and a small number of fans even insinuated that the Wildcats had purposely lost to Middle Tennessee in 1982 just to avoid having to face U of L. This time, Kentucky wasn't going to stand for such nonsense. The game was close from start to finish, but UK hung on to win, 64-59. Kentucky had done its part to set up the "Dream Game." Now the ball was in Louisville's court.

This Louisville-Arkansas game was just as close as that one in 1981, at least in the late stages. But at one point in the first half, the Razorbacks led 35-19. Gordon, the McCrays, and Wagner sparked a surge that brought the Cardinals back into contention. With the last 13 seconds ticking off the clock, the score was tied, 63-63, and U of L had possession. Crum signaled for a time-out to set up a shot for Wagner. His miss fell off into the hands of Jones and then Scooter McCray, whose tip-in just beat the final buzzer.

"I guess turnabout is fair play," Crum said. "Ours was a six-incher and theirs was a 50-footer, but they both count for two points."

On the floor, a Louisville cheerleader raised a fist

"You know, we really are great coaches," Denny Crum said to Jerry Jones as they walked off the floor after winning the season finale at Memphis State. "What do you mean, Coach?" Jones asked. "Jerry, didn't you realize that we didn't have anybody on the line when Milt (Wagner) was shooting those free throws? What if he had missed? There wasn't anybody under there to rebound. We didn't have anybody down there to tip or anything." Until then, neither Crum nor Jones had weighed the possibility of Wagner's not making the shots.

Milt Wagner

Souvenir Program $2.50

Mideast Regional • March 24-26, 1983
KNOXVILLE, TENNESSEE

Program cover from the 1983 Dream Game, which came about in the NCAA Mideast Regional championship game at Knoxville.

Louisville's players react to a rally that eventually led to victory over Kentucky in the 1983 Mideast Regional championship contest.

toward the Kentucky cheering section. "We want you!" he shouted. "Well, you got us!" a Kentucky cheerleader responded.

On the front page of a special section the next day in the *Louisville Times* was a gigantic headline stating "WAR!" On one side of the page was a picture of Joe B. Hall and on the other a photo of Denny Crum. But a headline in a much smaller paper told it even better: "Hell Freezes Over — They're Gonna Play."

For Louisville, things started going wrong from the start, when Wagner ran onto the floor as Gordon's name was called.

"In my mind, I thought we were better than Kentucky," Jerry Jones said. "We were better on paper, we were 31-3 and they were 21-7. But when the game started, Kentucky was awesome and we were plenty worried."

First, it became apparent that Charles Jones was having problems containing Kentucky's bulky center, Melvin Turpin. Also, Jim Master was proving to be a deadly shot from long range.

Kentucky took the early advantage and began pulling away. A basket by Derrick Hord gave the Cats their

Milt Wagner goes for an uncontested layup in 1983 against Kentucky.

biggest lead at 23-10. But with Scooter McCray hitting four of five from the field, Louisville closed the margin to 37-30 at halftime.

Just as Peck Hickman had ordered 24 years before, the first thing Louisville did to start the second half was to step up the intensity on defense. Kentucky raised the margin to 41-32, but the Louisville press was having its effect. The Wildcats were guilty of three straight turnovers, but a slam by Turpin allowed them to maintain their nine-point advantage at 45-36. Louisville was relentless in applying the pressure. Six straight points and it was 45-42. After a time-out, Coach Hall had his players try to throw over the press, and a long shot by Master kept Kentucky on top, 49-46.

The Cards kept coming, and Gordon finally pushed them in front at 50-49. And when Thompson connected from inside for a 58-53 lead, the Louisville crowd came to its feet in unison.

But Turpin and Master brought Kentucky back within a point at 58-57. Those two had been responsible for all of Kentucky's 20 second-half points. The Wildcats

Charles Jones (right) addresses the crowd while Lancaster Gordon (4) watches.

caught up at 60-60 with 3:09 to go when Charles Hurt tipped in a missed free throw.

Louisville turned the ball over, and Kentucky went into a freeze. With 49 seconds left, the score remained 60-60 and UK called for a time-out. With the clock ticking down under 20 seconds, Dirk Minniefield worked his way loose only to find Charles Jones there to intimidate his shot. That led to a go-ahead lay-up for Gordon.

Louisville's Lancaster Gordon is guarded by Charles Hurt of Kentucky.

With eight seconds to go and U of L now on top, 62-60, Kentucky took its final time-out. The idea was to hit Turpin inside, but instead the ball ended up in the capable hands of Master, who launched the tying basket from 10 feet, narrowly beating the final buzzer. The Dream Game was headed for overtime. Looking back, though, most Kentucky fans say they would have preferred that it had ended right there.

The end of Kentucky's dream began with a basket by Gordon. A steal, a basket, a UK miss, another basket, and by the time Kentucky finally scored, U of L had run off 14 points in a row. Just as in 1959, the Cards had blown it open at the end. It took a little longer this time, but the result was the same.

Louisville 80, Kentucky 68.

"At least for now, we *are* the University of Kentucky," Crum told cheering fans upon the team's return to Louisville.

But by the time practice began the following week, Jerry Jones could sense a difference. "It was as though a little of the edge was gone. Something we had in getting ready for Knoxville wasn't there now."

The Cards couldn't afford a letdown in the Final Four. Their semifinal opponent would be No. 1 Houston — Phi Slama Jama — with Akeem Olajuwon and Clyde Drexler.

The trip to New Mexico was rough. First, high winds seemed ready to flip the plane around as it bounced onto the runway in Albuquerque. Then there was the high altitude. Would it be a factor? Crum was constantly asked this question.

After North Carolina State upset Georgia in the first game, Louisville was primed and ready against Houston.

Denny Crum (center) poses with his coaching staff. Left to right are Bobby Dotson, Wade Houston, Crum, Tony Branch (graduate assistant) and Jerry Jones.

With 6:30 to go in the first half, U of L freshman Jeff Hall nailed a 22-footer from the baseline that pushed the Cardinals in front 29-27. By halftime, they had increased their advantage to 41-36.

The early portion of the second half looked even more promising, especially after Wagner's 20-footer at 13:15 gave Louisville its biggest lead of the afternoon, 57-49. But that's when the roof came crashing down. From that point, the Slama Jamas began slamming everything in sight. A slam by 6-2 Michael Young. One by Drexler. Another by Benny Anders. Three free throws and then another slam by Drexler. Two free throws by Young were offset by one from Rodney McCray. Then the Houston onslaught continued.

By the time the Cardinals regained their composure, Houston was ahead, 70-58. The final was 94-81. "They just physically overpowered us," Crum said. "It was an awesome display of force on their part."

Louisville closed with a 32-4 record, the second-highest victory total in the school's history. Some contend that only the altitude stopped the Cards from winning their second NCAA crown that year.

Then, too, is that other theory, something like an echo from a year gone by. "After Knoxville, maybe we were emotionally drained," said assistant coach Wade Houston. "Maybe beating Kentucky was enough."

Bobby Dotson

THE 1983-84 SEASON For the first time since 1922, Louisville and Kentucky played in a regular-season game. It happened at Kentucky's Rupp Arena on November 26, 1983. It was on that floor that the Cardinals would both begin and end their season.

Unfortunately for Louisville, now minus Rodney and Scooter McCray, the game came too early in the year. However, at season's end fate would give the Cards another shot. Kentucky, led by Kenny Walker, Melvin Turpin, and Sam Bowie, crushed U of L in Lexington 65-44 in the season-opener.

"I've been trying to tell the players they weren't ready," Crum said. "Now maybe they'll believe me."

Although there were some occasional lapses along the way, Crum's team would win 15 of 18 during one stretch. Victims included Iowa, North Carolina State, and UCLA. Two of the three setbacks came against Houston and tiny Chaminade in an eight-team tournament in Hawaii.

An injury to Billy Thompson in a 93-88 win at LaSalle on February 4 proved costly, and the Cardinals dropped three of their next four with the 6-8 sophomore on the sideline. But on February 18, Wagner scored 22 points and Louisville upset Memphis State (19-3 and unbeaten in

the Metro at the time), 75-68. Two weeks later, the Cards again beat the Tigers to close out the regular season at 21-9. Memphis State, however, gained a measure of revenge by winning the Metro Conference Tournament on its home floor after U of L was upset by Virginia Tech.

U of L started NCAA play in Milwaukee, where a sellout crowd watched Louisville beat Morehead, 72-59, with Jones scoring 33. The game with No. 12 Tulsa was a war from the very beginning. Louisville built a seemingly comfortable 65-54 lead with just under four minutes remaining. But Tulsa, led by Ricky Ross and Steve Harris, rallied to tie at 67-67. Then, with nine seconds left, Wagner calmly sank a jump shot to give Louisville a two-point victory and set up another game with No. 1 seed Kentucky.

Before 23,525 fans at Rupp Arena, where Kentucky had a 58-2 record over the previous four years, Louisville led the Wildcats 36-32 at halftime. The main reason was Lancaster Gordon, who finished with 25 points. The Cardinals continued to lead through much of the second half. But in the end, Kentucky rallied to win, 72-67.

The Wildcats went on to beat Illinois and reach the Final Four before losing to eventual champion Georgetown. And for Louisville, it wasn't such a bad year either.

THE 1984-85 SEASON A season that initially seemed full of promise quickly turned into a disaster. Entering the season, Crum's No. 1 concern was the development of 6-11 Barry Sumpter, the Cards' tallest player and also their least experienced.

Lancaster Gordon seems to be taking it easy while lying on the floor in front of the U of L bench. Doing the talking is assistant coach Jerry Jones.

"He's going to have to play, and the better he plays the better we'll be," Crum said at the time. "He's going to have to show improvement and be competitive if we're going to have a chance to do anything on a national scale."

However, Crum soon had other, more pressing concerns as injuries took a devastating toll that threatened to turn the year into a nightmare.

The most serious injury was to Milt Wagner's foot on December 1, 1984, in the dedication game of renovated Freedom Hall. It happened on a festive evening in front of the usual sellout crowd of 19,242. (Prior to the game with Virginia Commonwealth, Howard Schnellenberger received a standing ovation when he was introduced as the school's new football coach.)

Despite U of L's routine 67-55 victory, by the time the

Billy Thompson (55) battles teammate Pervis Ellison for a rebound during a preseason intrasquad game.

evening had ended, a dark cloud was hovering over the Cards' season: Wagner had suffered a broken fifth metatarsal in his right foot. Team physician Rudy Ellis was not optimistic that Wagner would be able to return that season. He was right. On December 2, a metal screw was inserted in Wagner's foot to hold a bone together, and he was through for the year.

It wasn't the last time Dr. Ellis and trainer Jerry May would be needed. Guard Kevin Walls underwent surgery to repair his right knee about a week later. Next, it was trouble in paradise. In the Cards' first game on a holiday trip to Hawaii they barely beat Hawaii-Hilo after coughing the ball up a record 38 times. They also lost their other starting guard, Jeff Hall, with an unusual injury. Taking a charge, Hall crashed to the floor and dislocated the fibula bone in his left leg.

U of L went on to lose three games in Hawaii, setting the tone for Crum's most disappointing year to that point. The Cards settled for an NIT bid, finishing fourth in that tournament with a 19-18 overall record. For the first time since his arrival at U of L in 1971, Crum failed to reach the coveted 20-win mark.

In an ironic twist, though, Wagner's injury set the stage for something few could envision in 1985 — a championship run the following year.

THE 1985-86 SEASON (NCAA CHAMPS AGAIN)

The operative word at the beginning of the season was "if."

"If" guard Milt Wagner could come back from the broken bone in his foot that had sidelined him for what would have been his senior season.

"If" senior forward Billy Thompson was finally able to become the superstar that most had expected when he signed in 1982.

"If" the rookie center, Pervis Ellison, could become an impact player in his first year.

Most agreed that the Cardinals would be good. With the return of Wagner and with Thompson back for one more shot, they would definitely have potential.

At center would be Ellison, provided the 6-9 freshman from Georgia progressed sufficiently in preseason practice. The forwards would be Thompson and sophomore Herbert Crook, both 6-7 experienced players who complemented each other well. The guards — Wagner and 6-2 senior Jeff Hall — were the Cards' strong suit, provided Wagner made a successful comeback. There was also excellent potential on the bench in muscular 6-7 forward Mark McSwain, and

CARDINALS QUIZ

23. In December 1957, U of L was host to the four-team Bluegrass Invitational. During the same month, Kentucky hosted its own four-team tourney. The third-place teams in each tournament would face each other later in the 1957-58 season. What were the teams and what were the circumstances of that game?

Herbert Crook

His knee heavily bandaged, Billy Thompson gets off a jump shot.

freshmen Tony Kimbro, Kenny Payne, and Kevin Walls.

Wagner was referred to as "Ice" by his teammates because he had always come through when the game was on the line. Just as the 1982-83 Final Four team had often displayed a quiet confidence exemplified by Rodney and Scooter McCray, this team would be confidently led by Wagner.

As for Thompson, he had arrived on campus in 1982 from Camden, N.J., labeled the top prospect in America.

"He had so much talent," recalled Hall. "We would watch him in practice and he would do something spectacular and we would stop and just marvel at this guy. But in the games, so many times it just wouldn't happen for him." But Thompson privately vowed to raise himself to the next level during his senior year. In so doing, he worked hard during the off-season, just as Darrell Griffith had done six years earlier.

As for the schedule, Crum always believed in playing the best. But in 1985-86 he may have outdone himself. For openers, there was the Big Apple NIT, including potential standout teams such as Kansas, Duke, and St. John's. Purdue, Indiana, Kentucky, UCLA, Syracuse, and North Carolina State were also on the agenda. So was Kansas in a regular-season game in Lawrence. And then, of course, there were Metro Conference games with Memphis State, Florida State, and Cincinnati.

U of L opened in Cincinnat's Riverfront Coliseum by defeating Miami of Ohio, 81-65, and Tulsa, 80-74, to earn its ticket to the NIT semifinals in New York. Awaiting the Cards were Larry Brown's Kansas Jayhawks, Duke, and St. John's. All of the Big Apple Final Four would later contend for the *real* Final Four in March. And three of this group would make it.

Milt Wagner was true to form on this play as he goes for an uncontested layup against Florida State's Seminoles.

Jeff Hall

Kansas beat the Cards, 83-78, and two nights later U of L dropped the third-place game to St. John's, 86-79. At this point, though, Crum wasn't all that upset with the team. After all, Wagner was still not at full strength and the season was very young.

The Cards then returned home and commenced a four-game winning streak with victories over Purdue, Iona, Western Kentucky, and Indiana. Next was a trip to Rupp Arena, where Louisville faced Eddie Sutton's 13th-ranked Kentucky Wildcats. This was the game the fans had to have, the season maker or breaker as far as they were concerned.

Crum didn't subscribe to this philosophy. A loss in December was a loss, regardless of the opposition. Make-or-break games are played in March. UK, led by Winston Bennett's 23 points, won, 69-64. But on the bright side for U of L, Wagner missed only four shots from the field and scored 19.

After the game, Sutton called Ellison perhaps the best freshman in the nation. "If I had to choose a freshman right now, he is who I would pick," he said. Louisville started the new year with easy victories over Wyoming and Eastern Kentucky and on January 9 initiated Metro Conference play at Memphis State. The Tigers were coming off a 1985 Final Four appearance and despite the loss of 6-10 Keith Lee, were still formidable foes. If the Cardinals weren't convinced before the game, they were after they lost, 73-71. "We gave it away at the free-throw line," Crum said.

On January 25, five days after a shocking 84-82 home loss to Metro rival Cincinnati, U of L limped into Lawrence for a rematch with the Kansas Jayhawks, who were now 18-2, compared with Louisville's somewhat disappointing 11-5 record.

After falling behind early, Louisville fought back hard and with seconds remaining gained possession under its basket, trailing 71-69. Thompson took the ball out of bounds and looked for Wagner, who later said he zigged when he should have zagged. Thompson's pass went out of bounds, and Kansas won the game. Afterward, Thompson was devastated. He appeared to be sulking, and at the airport and on the plane he isolated himself from the others, refusing to utter a word to anyone.

U of L was now 11-6, barely clinging to a spot in The Associated Press Top 25 and offering no clue that it could be a serious contender for the national championship. But Crum's team put together a mini-streak of four, all at Freedom Hall, by beating LaSalle, UCLA, South Carolina, and Virginia Tech. Against UCLA, Louisville led by only three at the half but won going away 91-72 as Wagner scored 20 and Thompson 16.

On February 8, Louisville journeyed to Raleigh to take on N.C. State before a national television audience. North Carolina State won 76-64, but it really wasn't that close. N.C. State's Ernie Myers said he was surprised at how soft Louisville's defense was. "I expected pressure like Duke's man-to-man, but it was easier," Myers said. In the Louisville dressing room, the players felt as though they had been reduced to mediocrity. "It was like we didn't even belong in the Top 25 and certainly weren't a title contender," Hall said. After the game, some of the players began to vent their frustrations.

Then, for one of the few times, Thompson spoke up. He had played possibly his best game of the year, scoring 21, missing only two shots and grabbing nine rebounds. "I'm tired of this. Let's go for it," Thompson said.

"If ever a loss was for the overall betterment of the team, that one was," Crum said later. "We were a different ball club after North Carolina State."

The Cardinals rolled to victories in their last nine regular-season games, but only after surviving scares in their final two in which they defeated South Carolina, 65-63, on the road and Memphis State, 70-69, at Freedom Hall. The latter came when "Ice" again lived up to his reputation by hitting a pair of free throws in the closing seconds.

The Metro Conference Tournament was played at Freedom Hall, and U of L defeated Cincinnati easily in the semifinal round and then polished off Memphis State, 88-79, in the championship game. Wagner scored 31 points and Ellison 21 in the finale.

Going into the NCAA, the team felt ready for the challenge. The tournament favorite was Duke, the top-seeded team in the East Regional and led by All-American Johnny Dawkins. Other top seeds were Kentucky in the Southeast, Kansas in the Midwest and St. John's in the West. Except for Duke, Louisville had played them all.

Louisville was assigned to the West Regional's first-round site in Ogden, Utah, where it was seeded No. 2 and paired against Drexel Institute of Philadelphia. "Must be one of them academic schools," Wagner said. With Thompson scoring 24 points and McSwain coming off the bench for 15, the Cards won without breaking a sweat, 93-73.

Two days later came confident Bradley, led by Hersey Hawkins. "U of L is one of those TV teams, the kind we want to play," said Bradley's Jim Les. Louisville, however, overcame a sluggish first half and advanced to the round of 16 by winning 82-68. The next stop was The Summit in Houston.

On the plane trip from Ogden back to Louisville,

CARDINALS QUIZ

24. *Louisville has had 14 consensus All-Americans. What player earned the honor most recently?*

CARDINALS QUIZ

25. *Who was the first U of L player to score more than 1,000 points during his career?*

Herbert Crook grabs a rebound despite being challenged by North Carolina's Warren Martin in 1986 NCAA Tournament action in Houston.

Herbert Crook, who had experienced subpar efforts against Drexel and Bradley, took a seat next to Crum. "Coach, I just want you to know this NCAA stuff is new to me," Crook said. "I didn't do much against those teams but things are gonna be different from here on out. You can write it on the wall." He lived up to his vow.

Louisville's first opponent in Houston was the No. 3 seed in the West, powerful North Carolina. Coach Dean Smith started a three-guard lineup, which Crum was able to exploit. U of L jumped ahead early, was tied at 43 at the half, then blew the game open in the final minutes and won, 94-79, as Thompson scored 24 and Crook 20.

The other game was won by Auburn, which upset UNLV. Auburn, Crum told his players, was possibly the most athletic team they had faced all year.

Again Louisville came from behind and by halftime the Cards had eased in front, 44-43. Louisville, switching late from a man-to-man to a zone defense, wrapped it up, 84-76. Crook scored 20, Wagner 16, Ellison 15, Hall 14, and Thompson 13. Once more Crum had a team going to the Final Four. This time the site was Reunion Arena in Dallas.

With the exception of surprising LSU, which had knocked off Kentucky to win the Southeast, the Final Four was the same group that had made up the semifinals at the Big Apple NIT in November. Only St. John's was missing.

Louisville was paired against LSU, and Duke again would play Kansas in a rematch of the Big Apple NIT championship game.

"We really thought we could beat Louisville," said LSU coach Dale Brown. "We peaked at the right time and everybody seemed to be overlooking us, which was just fine because never had I coached a more confident

Pervis Ellison (left) and Milt Wagner collect team and individual awards following Louisville's victory over Auburn in the final game of the 1986 NCAA West Regional Tournament at Houston.

*U of L's Billy
Thompson is hard
pressed to earn a
layup by David
Henderson of Duke
(12). At left are
Duke's Mark Alarie
(32) and Louisville's
Pervis Ellison (43)
and Jeff Hall (behind
Thompson).*

group of players. But it was like 1980 when we played
Louisville. Each team won a half. We won the first half,
but then it was as though someone turned out the lights
and they took us right out of the game."

LSU, led by Don Redden and Ricky Blanton, took an
early lead and was in front at intermission, 44-36. But
again the confident Cards came back to win, 88-77, and
moved into the championship game for the first time
since 1980. Thompson, hitting 10 of his 11 shots, and
Wagner each scored 22.

The day prior to the NCAA championship game,
most of Dallas and the national media were raving about
the Blue Devils and their star player, Johnny Dawkins.

Duke's win over Kansas had given it a record of 37-2, making it the winningest college team of all time.

"I remember reading an article in one of the papers the next day," Hall said. "The article went something like this: 'Duke has a beautiful campus with lots of ivory everywhere. They have an All-American in Johnny Dawkins, their other players are well mannered, they have the prettiest cheerleaders in the tournament, all the class you could want. The next national champion is Louisville.' "

It was apparent from the opening tip that Dawkins was going to be a formidable force. He scored eight of Duke's first nine points, and by the time he had 11 the Blue Devils were on top 25-18. Nothing would-be defenders Wagner, Tony Kimbro, and Kevin Walls could do seemed to matter. By halftime he had 17 and Duke maintained a narrow lead.

At 15:28, Dawkins lofted an 18-footer over Kimbro to

Milt Wagner snares a rebound while Duke's Mark Alarie (32) watches in the 1986 NCAA championship game between U of L and the Blue Devils. Behind Wagner is Duke superstar Johnny Dawkins.

Cardinal fans display their loyalty in the 1986 title game against Duke.

pad Duke's advantage to 48-42. At 10:08, he connected on another jump shot and the margin was 58-52. Little did the Duke faithful know that it would be the last field goal of Dawkins' college career.

With Hall now assigned to hawk the Duke star, the Cardinals began one last surge. When Wagner hit a lay-up with 3:22 to go, underdog Louisville finally went ahead at 64-63. Fourteen seconds later, Dawkins connected on two free throws and Duke momentarily regained the advantage. But Dawkins would score no more. He finished the night with 24.

"Up until then, I felt I had done very little to help the team in that game," Hall later confessed. "But once I started denying Dawkins the ball, I got this feeling of satisfaction, of doing a good job on a great player."

Thompson's eight-footer at 2:49 seesawed the Cardinals back to the front at 66-65. With 48 seconds to go, Crum called a time-out. His plan was for the guards, Wagner and Hall, to handle the ball as much as possible. If the shot was there, he wanted one of them to take it. Otherwise, wait until Duke fouled, because both were excellent free-throw shooters.

At 0:41 Hall saw his chance and put up an off-balance jump shot that he instantly knew was going to fall short. It was an air ball. Suddenly, out of the mass of players under the basket rose the long arms of Pervis Ellison to snatch the ball and place it perfectly in the basket. Louisville's lead was three. "I looked up and saw there wasn't anybody else around me. I was able to just go up, get it and lay it in," Ellison said.

In a couple of weeks, Hall would be asked about that air ball by the president of the United States. "Yes sir, it was the best air ball I ever shot," he told Ronald Reagan.

Duke came down the floor quickly, missed a hasty shot and Ellison was fouled on the rebound. With only 27 seconds showing on the clock, the freshman lived up to his nickname of "Never Nervous" Pervis and sank them both. Now Louisville led by five.

In desperation, Duke scored and then immediately fouled Thompson, who missed the front end of the one-and-one. It wasn't quite over yet. Tommy Amaker's lay-up sliced it to 70-69 with 12 seconds to go.

With 17,007 fans screaming, Wagner was fouled with seven seconds left, and "Ice" stepped to the line. Laughing, he knew it was all over. No crowd, no opponent, no pressure. Nothing could stop him now.

He sank them both, and for the 10th time during the year, Louisville had come from behind to win after trailing at halftime. Far more important, for the second time in the '80s, U of L reigned as champion of the collegiate basketball kingdom.

Ellison was U of L's leading scorer against Duke with

Louisville players proudly display the 1986 NCAA championship trophy they won by beating Duke, 72-69.

One of the rewards the NCAA champion receives is an invitation to visit the President of the United States at the White House. Here, President Ronald Reagan greets members of the U of L team.

25 points, including 10 of 14 from the field, and was named Most Valuable Player of the Final Four, marking the first time since Arnie Ferrin of Utah in 1944 that such an honor was bestowed upon a freshman.

Pervis was joined on the All-Final Four team by teammate Billy Thompson and Johnny Dawkins, Tommy Amaker, and Mark Alarie of Duke.

Backing up his words at N.C. State with action, Thompson had hit an incredible 70 percent of his shots from the field in U of L's six NCAA Tournament games. Suddenly, all the critics were gone.

THE 1986-87 SEASON Despite high national rankings and expectations going into the season, Crum foresaw major problems.

This was the first year for the three-point rule in college basketball, and U of L was woefully short on outside marksmen.

Ellison and junior forward Herbert Crook were the only returning starters, and Crum also suspected that the Cards were complacent in the aftermath of their second title. He called the preseason accolades "ridiculous."

In what was to become known as "The Great Alaska Shutout," U of L lost all three games in the season-opening eight-team tournament in Anchorage. And the losses did not come against top-caliber competition. Instead, the Cards fell victims to lightweights Northeastern, Washington, and Texas.

When they returned to the Lower 48, things improved — but not for long. It would be a topsy-turvy

Former Cardinal Butch Beard looks at ex-teammate Wes Unseld while giving a speech at a team reunion.

year cluttered with many disappointments and few highlights. Perhaps the most embarrassing moment was in an 85-51 blowout loss to Kentucky at Freedom Hall. Almost as bad was a 99-71 thrashing at Syracuse. Yet the team won the regular-season Metro Conference title with a 9-3 league record.

After a roller-coaster season, U of L finished with an 18-14 overall record, capped by a sleepwalking 75-52 loss to archrival Memphis State in Freedom Hall in the championship game of the Metro Conference Tournament.

The Cards were then snubbed by the NCAA Selection Committee, which frowned on the idea that Memphis State, barred from the NCAA Tournament by probation, had been allowed to participate in the Metro tourney.

Louisville's exclusion from the 64-team field infuriated Crum. Instead of handling such adversity in his usual mild-mannered way, he called the decision "a slap at the Metro Conference." In a team vote, the Cards chose — barely — to accept an NIT bid. But because the players were less than enthusiastic about it, Crum decided to reject the invitation. The decision broke a string of 21 consecutive postseason appearances for Louisville.

"They're going to go to class, and I'm going to go fishing," he fumed.

CARDINALS QUIZ

26. Who was the most recent U of L player to reach the 1,000-point mark?

THE 1987-88 SEASON U of L's only question mark when the season started was inexperience at guard, and the pollsters apparently didn't see that as much of a problem, putting the Cards anywhere from seventh to 20th in the preseason

Kevin Walls, one of Crum's Camden Connection players in 1985-86, signals for a play. Walls later left the team, citing lack of playing time as the major reason.

rankings. Undoubtedly, that was because U of L had a solid front line with forwards Kenny Payne and Herbert Crook, and centers Pervis Ellison and Felton Spencer. The backcourt spots went to sophomore Keith Williams and freshman LaBradford Smith.

U of L wobbled out of the gate in the Big Four Classic in Indianapolis, suffering a 69-54 thrashing at the hands of Notre Dame. Smith's heralded debut turned into a disaster that produced five turnovers, five fouls, and one-of-five field goal shooting.

"We were basket cases out there," Crum said.

That left U of L fans to wonder just how bad the

carnage would be in U of L's next appearance — against top-ranked Kentucky in Rupp Arena. Twenty points? Thirty points? More?

Trailing 45-32 at halftime and on the verge of the blowout that everyone expected, U of L rallied to tie the score at 65-65 on Smith's free throw with 5:03 left. Ellison put U of L ahead 75-74 on a 10-footer at 0:39, but Cedric Jenkins' tip-in of a missed shot by Ed Davender at 0:02 gave UK a 76-75 victory.

A few days after the loss, U of L got some more bad news — junior forward Tony Kimbro, who had started all 32 games in 1986-87, was ordered by the school to sit out the season because of academic problems.

However, in the next game against a ranked opponent, U of L overcame a 10-point halftime deficit to stun No. 5 Indiana, 81-69, behind Smith's 32 points. Smith, who also had five rebounds and three assists, hit all 14 of his free throws to run his string to 25.

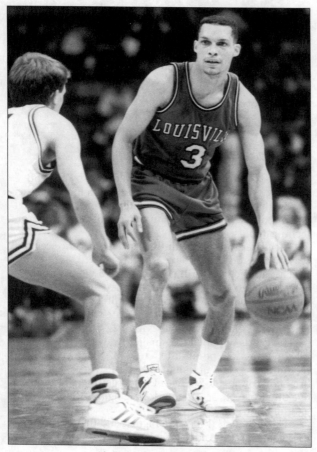

Keith Williams

Herbert Crook goes for a layup while four Memphis State players watch.

A 20-10 regular season was highlighted by a 98-88 double-overtime victory at South Carolina in which the Cards trailed by 14 with 70 seconds left in regulation, at which point a brawl broke out that resulted in numerous technical fouls.

They later took their ninth Metro Conference regular season title and sixth league tourney crown.

The latter came during a sweet 81-73 victory over Memphis State, the Cards' first tourney title on the Tigers' homecourt in five tries. So U of L, which once stood 10-8, headed into its NCAA date with Oregon State in The Omni in Atlanta with a 22-10 record.

The Cards whipped the smaller Beavers, 70-61, as Ellison scored 23 points and Crook 22. Each collected 11 rebounds. Next, U of L manhandled 19th-ranked Brigham Young, 97-76, with Ellison getting 24 points, five other players scoring in double figures, and Williams handing out 12 assists.

"They're taller, they jump higher, and they're quicker," BYU coach Ladell Andersen said. "They lost 10 games, so

Will Olliges of Louisville battles a UCLA player in a 1988 game at Freedom Hall which the Cardinals won, 92-79.

evidently they don't play that way all the time."

That set up a showdown with top-seeded, fourth-ranked Oklahoma (33-2) in the Southeast semifinals in Birmingham. The run-and-gun, pressing Sooners proved to be too much for the Cards, who trailed only 55-51 at halftime but committed seven turnovers in the first 4:43 of the second half, lost the ball on four of their first five possessions, and never recovered in falling 108-98.

THE 1988-89 SEASON With Ellison, Kenny Payne, LaBradford Smith, Keith Williams, and Felton Spencer back, plus the return of Tony Kimbro from academic hiatus, the Cards appeared to be poised for a serious run at the national championship.

"I think this team is just as talented as the '86 team," said Ellison, who was trying to stage an encore after leading U of L in scoring (17.6), rebounding (8.3), blocked shots (102), and field-goal percentage (.601) as a junior.

U of L was ranked fourth in the AP's preseason poll,

LaBradford Smith

and with the Cards playing in the Big Apple NIT, many
fans expected to spend Thanksgiving in New York City.
But Xavier spoiled the planned holiday by shocking the
Cards, 85-83, in their season debut in Riverfront
Coliseum in Cincinnati. Louisville — playing without
academically sidelined starting guard Keith Williams —
made 33 errors.

Vanderbilt's Barry Goheen handed the Cards another
heartbreaking loss, 65-62, on a 45-foot "Hail Barry" shot
at the buzzer in Nashville. "I just threw it up and hoped
for the best," Goheen said.

U of L turned things around in its next game against
Indiana in the Big Four Classic in Indianapolis. Under
orders from Crum to quit pressing and start having fun,
the Cards smothered the Hoosiers with full-court
pressure, jumped to a 9-0 lead, and romped, 101-79. IU
didn't get a shot in its first five possessions.

The triumph sparked a 14-game winning streak
highlighted by a 97-75 bashing of Kentucky on New
Year's Eve that snapped a three-game losing streak

against the Wildcats.

"Louisville is the best team we've played in the four years I've been at Kentucky," UK coach Eddie Sutton said.

In late January, U of L notched another impressive win, rolling up a 22-point halftime lead en route to a 92-74 thumping of No. 11 UNLV as Ellison hit 10 of 11 shots and equaled his career high with 28 points.

CARDINALS QUIZ

The Cards inched up to No. 3 in the AP poll, and losses by top-ranked Illinois and No. 2 Georgetown put them in position to claim the top spot going into a home game against No. 17 Ohio State on January 29.

27. *True or False. Louisville has never finished second in either the NIT or the NCAA tournaments.*

In one swoop that day, U of L lost its chance at No. 1, its 14-game winning streak, and its heart and soul. Ellison suffered a sprained ligament in his left knee with 44 seconds remaining in the first half and was forced to the sidelines indefinitely. The Cards led 41-37 at intermission, but Jay Burson's 29 points and seven rebounds led the Buckeyes to an 85-79 upset.

That game was to mark the turning point in U of L's season. Although Ellison missed only two games — both victories — the Cards were never the same. In Ellison's first game back, the Cards lost, 81-78, to Florida State in Freedom Hall — the beginning of a slump that resulted in five losses in eight games.

Included were two defeats that are among the most memorable in U of L history. First came an ill-fated trip to Los Angeles, where a disputed goaltending call against Ellison on a late shot by Pooh Richardson gave UCLA a 77-75 victory.

"I doubt that there is even a UCLA fan in here who feels that was goaltending," Crum fumed afterward.

A day later, though, after reviewing the tape of the play, referee Willis McJunkin was adamant. "I don't have any qualms about my call whatsoever," he said. "I wouldn't change a thing."

U of L had another close call in its next outing, but this time freshman guard Everick Sullivan drilled a baseline three-pointer at the buzzer for a 78-77 overtime win at Florida State.

Pervis Ellison

The Cards' previous four games had been decided by a total of nine points, and the next one was close, too — although it didn't start out that way. Memphis State — in what Crum later referred to as an "absolute joke" — raced to a 24-0 lead in Freedom Hall, then held on for a 72-67 win.

U of L also lost two of its next three games, despite lineup changes that sent Kimbro and Williams to the bench and Spencer and Sullivan into starting roles, with Ellison moving to forward. But the Cards regrouped to beat Notre Dame and win the Metro tourney in Columbia, S.C., by edging Memphis State on Sullivan's free throw at 0:02 and downing Florida State, 87-80.

Seeded No. 4 in the Midwest Regional and ranked 12th nationally, U of L defeated Arkansas-Little Rock and Arkansas in the Hoosier Dome in Indianapolis. Against the Hogs, Smith turned in the best all-around performance of his collegiate career, collecting 26 points, eight assists, four rebounds and three steals.

Looming next was top-seeded and third-ranked Illinois (29-4) in another dome — the Metrodome in Minneapolis. The Cards seemed to get a break when Illinois senior forward Ken Battle was unable to start because of a knee injury. But U of L soon had injury problems of its own when Ellison collided with Illini forward Marcus Liberty just 2½ minutes into the game and went out with a

After helping U of L to the 1986 national championship, Pervis Ellison became one of only two freshmen ever voted the MVP of the Final Four. Later, he was the only Cardinal ever chosen No. 1 in the NBA draft — by the Sacramento Kings in 1989. Ellison now plays for the Boston Celtics.

bruised knee. Seconds later, Illinois center Lowell Hamilton retired to the bench with a sprained ankle.

Ellison wasn't seriously hurt but said his effectiveness was hampered. Making several short trips to the bench to ice his knee, he wound up with 12 points, nine rebounds, and seven blocked shots. But he scored only one basket in the second half.

Still, U of L stayed in contention until the final 2:05 when Illinois put the game away by scoring six straight points to boost a 73-66 lead to 79-66. The final score was 83-69.

THE 1989-90 SEASON Even though U of L posted a 27-8 record, won both the Metro Conference regular-season and tournament championships, and made another appearance in the Sweet Sixteen, the way this season ended left a bitter taste in Crum's mouth.

Considered a Final Four candidate after finishing the regular campaign on a roll, U of L stumbled in the second round of the NCAA Tournament, losing a 62-60 shocker to Ball State in the West Regional in Salt Lake City.

"I don't get upset with losses, but I hate to get beat when we don't play our best," said Crum, whose team trailed from start to finish.

Felton Spencer

Otherwise, the season was a success, with Crum notching 20 victories for the 17th time despite losing two key players — top NBA draft choice Pervis Ellison and another first-round NBA pick, Kenny Payne — from the 1989 club.

THE 1990-91 SEASON It was amazing. Here was the worst U of L team ever under Crum and the Cards were within minutes of earning the Metro Conference's automatic NCAA Tournament bid, which would have sent them into the tourney with a 15-15 record.

But it wasn't to be. Leading Florida State by 20 points four minutes into the second half in the title game in Roanoke, Va., the Cards ran out of gas and lost, 76-69.

U of L finished 14-16, ending its NCAA-record string of consecutive winning seasons at 46. The school's last losing mark was 7-10 in 1941-42. U of L didn't have a team in 1942-43, was 10-10 in 1943-44, then started its streak with a 16-3 record in 1944-45.

"That's life," Crum said. "You can't change it. When it's over, it's over."

U of L was left shorthanded when four standout recruits — Dwayne Morton, Greg Minor, Brian Hopgood, and Anthony Cade — failed to qualify academically and Jerome Harmon left school two years early.

It was also a tumultuous season off the court for Crum. He publicly battled with U of L President Donald Swain

Despite playing only three years, Greg Minor joined the list of 1,000-point scorers at U of L with a total of 1,199 from '91-92 through '93-94. He also ranks seventh in career 3-point goals with 94. He now plays for the Boston Celtics.

over academic standards; took on *60 Minutes* for an extremely unfavorable — and unfair — report about the academic record of U of L basketball players during the 1980s; and even took part in a demonstration staged by the school's coaches over distribution of the money U of L received from its Fiesta Bowl football appearance against Alabama. Crum and the coaches felt too much was being funneled into minority programs instead of athletics.

THE 1991-92 SEASON The battle cry for this season was: "From Worst to First." They almost made it, winding up in a three-way tie for second in the Metro, just one game behind Tulane.

The season brought the long-awaited debut of Greg Minor and Dwayne Morton, a pair of outstanding recruits who had to sit out 1990-91 for academic reasons. They were among three newcomers — the other was freshman guard Keith LeGree — to the starting lineup.

CARDINALS QUIZ

28. Name two former U of L players who became head coaches of NBA teams.

Crum, 54 and in his 21st year of coaching U of L, signed a five-year contract extension on December 19, 1991, a few hours before Morton scored 33 points to spark his club past Morehead State, 90-76, in Freedom Hall. The new pact took Crum through the 1997-98 season.

Two days later the hero was LeGree, who swished a leaning three-pointer from well beyond the top of the key to lift the Cards to a 93-92 victory over LSU in Baton Rouge and overcome a 22-point, 14-rebound, six-block performance by 7-1 Shaquille O'Neal.

"It looked to me like everybody was just running around," LeGree said. "Corn (Cornelius Holden) got the ball to me, I looked up and just shot it."

The win sent No. 21 U of L into its showdown with No. 17 Kentucky (7-2) on December 28 in Rupp Arena with a 6-0 record. But the Cards crashed hard. Hitting 11 of 21 three-point shots, UK blistered U of L, 103-89.

"Our lack of communication on defense hurt us more than anything else," Crum said. "We didn't do a good job of helping each other."

U of L dropped its first two Metro games to Tulane and VCU and had a five-game losing streak on the road dating to the previous season. So it didn't look good when the Cards headed for Lawrence, where Kansas awaited with the nation's No. 4 ranking, an 11-0 record, and a 30-game non-conference winning streak in Allen Fieldhouse.

Improbable as it was, the Cards shocked Kansas, 85-78, as Crum simplified the offense, in many cases isolating Morton to go one-on-one. Morton played only 17 minutes due to foul trouble, but still led U of L with 20 points, and sophomore guard Kip Stone came off the bench to score a career-best 12 points.

A modest four-game winning streak ensued, capped by the school's 1,200th victory in its 78th season, an 88-74 triumph over Southern Miss in Freedom Hall in which the Cards drilled nine of 14 threes.

U of L was struggling when it went West, having dropped four of its previous seven games, and it looked as if another setback was imminent when Arizona State forged a 15-point lead with 14:02 left. But the Cards held the Sun Devils to a mere four points in the final 14 minutes of regulation, then escaped 63-62 in overtime, with Sullivan's two free throws at 1:17 providing the winning margin.

"They were phenomenal in the second half," ASU coach Bill Frieder said.

The Cards weren't phenomenal often enough the rest of the way. VCU stunned U of L, 74-65, in the first round of the Metro Tournament in Freedom Hall, denying the Cards a seventh straight trip to the championship game, handing them their first first-round loss since 1976 and putting them on the bubble for the NCAA Tournament with an 18-10 record.

U of L made the field, was seeded eighth and sent back to Tempe to meet No. 9 Wake Forest in the West Regional. To neutralize the Demon Deacons' superior size inside, Crum dusted off a rarely-used 2-3 zone and the Cards walloped Wake, 81-58, their largest margin in an NCAA Tournament game since an 81-52 rout of Middle Tennessee in 1982. Morton led the way with 20 points and 10 rebounds.

That set up a rematch with fourth-ranked, top-seeded UCLA (26-4), which had beaten U of L 78-64 in

CARDINALS QUIZ

29. Two of Louisville's longtime opponents have particularly dismal records against the Cardinals, having each lost 51 contests. What schools are they?

Dwayne Morton came to Louisville after the Cards won a recruiting battle with Kentucky coach Rick Pitino. Here, Morton goes for a layup against the Wildcats.

Louisville on February 2. This one was virtually a replay, with the Bruins controlling the game from start to finish as the Cards were unable to handle the M&M boys, Don MacLean and Tracy Murray, who scored 26 and 23 points respectively. Working the ball inside and drawing fouls, UCLA hit 35 of 43 free throws, including 34 of 41 in the second half and won, 85-69.

Afterward Crum promised: "We will be back."

THE 1992-93 SEASON This season was notable for the debut of 6-9 sophomore center Clifford Rozier, one of the nation's top recruits when he signed with North Carolina out of Southeast High School in Bradenton, Fla., and the first transfer Crum had taken in his 22 years at Louisville.

Rozier immediately became a key cog in the Cards' machine and had another outstanding season as a junior before becoming another first for Crum — his first player to leave early for the NBA.

In teaming with Dwayne Morton and Greg Minor to lead the Cards to a 22-9 record, Rozier produced 18 scoring and rebounding double-doubles, was named Metro Conference Player of the Year and became the first

U of L player to average in double figures in rebounding (10.9) in 21 years. He also averaged 15.7 points.

This was also the first year that the three-point shot made a significant impact for the Cards, who set season and single-game school records for threes made and attempted and ranked sixth nationally (180-427, 41.6 percent) in three-point accuracy.

U of L started slowly, losing four of its first six games, including a 90-88 setback at Vanderbilt on a rebound basket by center Chris Lawson with one second remaining and an 88-68 drubbing at the hands of Kentucky in Freedom Hall. It was U of L's worst homecourt loss since an 85-51 whipping by UK in 1986.

"My compliments to Kentucky," Crum said. "They played about as well as you can play at both ends of the floor. ... It seemed like they hit everything they threw up."

Not quite, but close. The Wildcats made 11 of 21 threes to U of L's two of 10.

After losing two of their next three, the Cards finally started to click, hammering Oral Roberts, 122-76, to start a string of 11 wins in 12 games, the only loss coming at home against No. 4 Kansas, 98-77. Against Oral Roberts, senior guard James "Boo" Brewer set a school record by hitting eight three-pointers (in 14 tries) and U of L set a team mark with 16 of 30. The total points fell just shy of the record of 126 set by the 1971-72 club against St. Peter's.

Crum reached another personal milestone on January 7 in Tampa, when the Cards ripped South Florida, 98-75, to hand him his 500th career victory behind Rozier's 25 points, 13 rebounds and four blocked shots. Crum reached 500 faster than any coach other than Jerry Tarkanian.

"I'm glad it's behind us," Crum said. "It's a nice feeling to be there; now we can concentrate on other things. When you start the season knowing it's close, you wonder how long it's going to take."

U of L was 13-6 when it visited UNLV (16-2), which owned the nation's longest homecourt winning streak at 59 and hadn't lost at the Thomas and Mack Center since Oklahoma won, 90-88, on January 28, 1989.

"I told the players before the game that they had a golden opportunity," Crum said. "I told them that if they gave their maximum effort, it was within the realm of their ability to beat this team."

They did, 90-86.

Morton was superb. He collected a season-high 29 points and eight rebounds, and also had three assists, a blocked shot, a steal and no turnovers in 33 minutes.

Morton went from hero to goat two days later when he missed a dunk just before the buzzer in a 78-77 loss to Western Kentucky in Freedom Hall. The Cards had beaten the Hilltoppers 14 in a row and hadn't lost to

CARDINALS QUIZ

30. What team holds the record for most lifetime victories over the Cardinals?

them since 1961.

After a loss at Houston, U of L ended the season with four straight wins. Included was one fans will always remember, but not because of the game. A snow and ice storm held the crowd for a February 25 win over North Carolina Charlotte to just 7,149 hardy souls. It was the smallest turnout since 6,872 witnessed a 66-57 victory over Georgetown College on December 2, 1972.

U of L thumped Tulane, 94-67, to clinch its 11th Metro crown and end a two-year drought. Its 11-1 conference record was its best since a 12-0 mark in 1982-83. The Cards also won the Metro tourney and were seeded No. 4 in the NCAA Midwest Regional in the Hoosier Dome in Indianapolis.

U of L was ragged in its NCAA opener, squandering most of an 18-point lead against 13th-seeded Delaware before holding on for a 76-70 victory. Next came Oklahoma State and the Cowboys' 7-foot, 285-pound center, Bryant "Big Country" Reeves, who led the Big Eight in scoring (19.7), rebounding (10.1), and field-goal shooting (62.4 percent) while earning Player of the Year honors in the league.

Rozier proved equal to the task, getting 19 points and eight rebounds, while Reeves finished with 14 points and nine boards, as U of L rallied in the second half for a 78-63 victory and a trip to St. Louis to meet top-ranked Indiana (30-3) in the regional semifinals. "I don't know if I've ever had a team outscored like that," Eddie Sutton said.

A week later, Louisville couldn't stop IU All-American Calbert Cheaney, who tossed in 32 points in the Hoosiers' 82-69 victory. The smooth senior forward hit 10 of 12 shots and also had four assists.

"Calbert Cheaney is awesome," Crum said. "We didn't have anyone who could guard him."

THE 1993-94 SEASON With its best inside-outside balance in years, U of L put together two 10-game winning streaks en route to its best record (28-6) since the 1982-83 Final Four club finished 32-4.

Off the court it was a big year for Crum, who became one of only three active coaches to be elected to the Naismith Basketball Hall of Fame, joining North Carolina's Dean Smith and Indiana's Bob Knight.

Rookies Jason Osborne and DeJuan Wheat both started against UK, marking the first time two freshmen had started an opener for Crum. They remained in the lineup the whole year, with Osborne's 4.1 assists per game good for third in the Metro. He also averaged 9.6 points, and Wheat contributed 12.6 points and 3.2 assists.

U of L opened the season ranked No. 7, but once again Kentucky had the Cards' number. This time the

CARDINALS QUIZ

31. U of L has played this team five times in NCAA play and once in the NIT. Who is it?

score was 78-70 as UK overcame a big game by Rozier to win its fourth straight in the series. Rozier had game highs of 29 points, 13 rebounds, and three blocks, but Osborne and Wheat had typical rookie jitters. Wheat scored only six points on one-of-eight shooting and Osborne missed all six of his field goal attempts and committing six turnovers.

"We played terrible, that's all there is to it," Rozier said. "Kentucky left their hearts on the court."

U of L was to fall only once more in the next 2½ months, a 93-89 homecourt overtime loss to VCU. Rozier had an even better game a couple of weeks after the UK loss, hitting all 15 of his field-goal attempts against Eastern Kentucky to tie the NCAA record shared by nine others, including former Card Cornelius Holden (14 of 14 at Southern Miss on March 3, 1990).Rozier wound up with 32 points and 13 rebounds in the 90-66 romp.

"Cliff put on a *Masterpiece Theater* performance," said Matt Simons, Rozier's backup.

But despite a 20-2 record, all wasn't well. Crum complained that the Cards weren't as intense as they had been earlier in the year and weren't improving. Following U of L's 10th straight win, 77-73 over Tulane, he called his players cocky and inattentive, and said that coaching them had ceased to be fun. He also said that they didn't have what it takes to win a championship.

"They look awfully good to me," Tulane coach Perry Clark said. "Maybe he's talking about the NBA championship instead of the NCAA title."

"We're playing like dogs," Crum said. "Our guys don't have a clue how you get to the Final Four. They think just showing up is all you have to do. It would probably be really good for us to get beat so I could get their attention again."

Less than a week later, Crum got his wish. Unranked North Carolina Charlotte, a 21-point victim in Freedom Hall two weeks earlier, upset No. 5 U of L, 64-62, for its first victory over a top 10 team since 1977.

But the loss didn't have the results Crum desired. The Cards followed with another lackluster performance in losing to Temple, 68-63, in the 7-Up Shootout in Orlando. Rozier, who said his back hurt from a spill he took at UNCC, took only one shot and scored just one point.

U of L won four straight after that, then ended the regular season with a 75-72 loss at No. 15 UCLA, which moved to 7-0 over U of L in Pauley Pavilion.

U of L appeared headed for an upset loss in its opening game of the Metro tourney against Virginia Tech. But at halftime Crum benched starters Morton, Wheat, and Osborne and the Cards overcame a 14-point deficit to win, 76-67.

CARDINALS QUIZ

32. Louisville hold a 3-0 record in NCAA Tournament play against this team.

Cliff Rozier

"I was surprised," Osborne said. "Coach Crum was very irate. That's the maddest I've seen him all year."

U of L again had what Crum called a "horrible" first half in the final the next night against Southern Miss, but prevailed 69-61 to capture its 10th tourney title. The Cards (26-5) were seeded No. 3 and paired against Big Sky Tournament champ Boise State (17-12) in the NCAA West Regional in Sacramento.

With their heads freshly shaved, the Cards built a 49-27 lead, then survived a scare to hold off Boise State, 67-58.

The Cards had another close shave in their next game, scrambling from 12 points down to overtake Minnesota, 60-55, and advance to the regional semifinals in Los Angeles against No. 2 seed Arizona (27-5).

"We've not gotten any credit for our defense," Crum

Louisville's 1994-95 Cardinal Bird, Aaron Flaker, won the NCAA competition for best mascot during competition in Dallas. The following year, the Cardinal cheerleaders won their sixth national crown in 11 years.

said. "Nobody thinks of Louisville playing defense, but defense is what has carried us. When you only score 60 points you probably shouldn't win at this level. I don't think we can get by any of the teams remaining unless we play a lot better than we have the last few."

They didn't. They couldn't stop Arizona guard Khalid Reeves and couldn't solve their recent shooting woes. Reeves burned U of L for 29 points and four other players scored in double figures. Morton scored 21, but Rozier was held to five points. He got his only field goal in the first minute and was zero for three the rest of the way. U of L missed 13 of its first 16 shots and finished at 37.3 percent, including seven of 27 from three-point range.

"You've got to make your shots, and we couldn't get the ball in the hole," Crum said. "That'll get you beat every night."

CARDINALS QUIZ

33. Six players have led U of L in scoring three successive years. Who are they?

THE 1994-95 SEASON With Clifford Rozier departing early for the NBA and Greg Minor and Dwayne Morton having exhausted their eligibility, Crum had his youngest team ever. U of L didn't have a senior on its roster, and the Cards played like it, riding a roller coaster to a 19-14 season that ended with their first opening-round loss in the NCAA Tournament since 1981. The inexperience showed up particularly in close games, with six losses coming by four points or fewer.

Easily the highlight of the season came on New Year's Day against Kentucky. Unranked U of L (6-3) had lost four in a row to UK and was given little chance of ending the streak against the sixth-ranked Cats (6-1), even though the game was played in Freedom Hall.

However, the Cards showed their moxie with an 88-86 upset, as Samaki Walker blocked a school-record 11 shots in achieving the only triple-double in U of L history (he also had 14 points and 10 rebounds).

"I couldn't see me going four years here and not beating Kentucky," said DeJuan Wheat, who turned in a superb all-around effort with 23 points, five assists, four rebounds, and three steals. "I wanted to get that taken care of right now."

The turning point came after UK had grabbed a 54-49 lead at the 13:48 mark. Wheat hit three straight outside jumpers, including back-to-back threes, during a 14-2 burst that put the Cards back in control. Wheat also hit the clinching free throws with less than one second left in the game after a three-pointer by Walter McCarty had pulled the Cats to within 86-84.

"To me, that's what college basketball is all about," Crum said. "It's a shame someone had to lose, because both teams played well enough to win. I would have been proud of my team if we had lost because they

Greg Minor

played their hearts out."

The toughest stretch of the season came in February when they dropped four straight while Walker was sidelined with a stress fracture in his foot, but the low point was a shocking 81-69 loss to Towson State (8-9) on January 30 in Baltimore. The Tigers, 2-6 in the Big South Conference and losers to such no-names as Winthrop, Radford and Liberty, limited U of L to 42.6 percent shooting, forced 20 turnovers and held the Cards to one field goal in the final 4:53.

When Walker returned, he got 15 points and eight rebounds as the Cards defeated VCU, 80-64, but they ended the regular season with a 91-73 homecourt loss to UCLA and limped into the Metro tourney with a 16-13 record.

Needing to win the Metro for the league's automatic NCAA Tournament berth or be shut out of the field, the Cards swept to three victories in little more than 36 hours in Freedom Hall, beating VCU (84-61), Tulane (81-80 in overtime), and Southern Miss (78-64). It

DeJuan Wheat

marked the swan song for the 20-year-old Metro, which was merged with the Great Midwest to form Conference USA for the 1995-96 season.

Although they were impressive in the Metro tourney, the Cards had a short stay in the NCAA. Seeded 11th in the Midwest Regional in Austin, Texas, they were hammered by archrival and No. 6 seed Memphis, 77-56.

"Memphis physically dominated us every way they could dominate us," Crum said.

THE 1995-96 SEASON There had never been another season like this, and the circumstances certainly weren't ones Crum would have picked to help him celebrate his silver anniversary at U of L. Yet, as stressful and tumultuous as the year was, it also proved to be one of the coach's most gratifying because of the hustle, grit, and determination his players exhibited under almost constant adversity and distractions.

The Doctors of Spunk, as they became known, became one of the school's most popular teams. They overcame academic ineligibilities, injuries, suspensions, the resignation of assistant coach Larry Gay, and an ongoing NCAA investigation to post a 22-12 record, beat four Top 25 teams, lose to five others by a total of 11 points, and advance to the Sweet Sixteen.

In so doing, the Cards beat all odds and will be remembered fondly as true overachievers. For much of the year, U of L played without four potential starters — forward Jason Osborne, swingman Eric Johnson, center Samaki Walker, and center/forward Alex Sanders.

The victories included two improbable upsets on enemy courts — a 72-66 win at sixth-ranked Cincinnati and a 78-76 buzzer-beater at 15th-ranked and defending national champion UCLA.

Before the season got under way, the news was all bad. Osborne, a junior and a two-year starter, and Sanders, a highly recruited 6-7 sophomore who had sat out the 1994-95 season for academic reasons, were declared academically ineligible for the first semester. And the 6-9 Walker, the Metro Conference Freshman of the Year with averages of 13.7 points and 7.2 rebounds, was suspended for the first two games for a secondary NCAA violation. Starting guard Tick Rogers also missed the first two games with a broken bone in his shooting hand.

Then, in the second game of the season against Virginia Commonwealth in the San Juan Shootout, Johnson suffered a knee injury and was lost for the year.

As it turned out, neither Osborne or Sanders would play at all, and Osborne left school at the end of the spring semester. Walker wound up missing 13 games, including one with a sprained ankle and 10 while

CARDINALS QUIZ

34. Only one Conference USA team holds a lifetime series advantage against U of L. Name the team.

CARDINALS QUIZ

35. This former star player for U of L had his number retired after a 10-year career with the Milwaukee Bucks. Who is he?

CARDINALS QUIZ

36. This former star player for the Cardinals enjoyed immediate success in the NBA and was named Rookie of the Year. When he retired after 10 season as a pro, he had scored 12,391 points. Who is he?

awaiting an NCAA ruling on his acquistion of a car. Surprisingly, U of L was 11-2 without him in the lineup.

U of L was 2-2 going into its home debut against Michigan State when the players held a team meeting that they credited with igniting a 79-59 rout. Crum used a zone defense from start to finish for the first time in his career, and Alvin Sims led the Cards with 17 points, seven steals, four rebounds, three assists, and two blocks.

That paved the way for a four-game winning streak that featured a 101-78 romp past Texas in Freedom Hall as Walker collected a career-high 17 rebounds and also scored 15 points. Junior walk-on B.J. Flynn — exhibiting the all-out hustle that was to become his trademark — came off the bench to deliver 17 points, four rebounds, three assists, and two steals. U of L was up 18-0 after 3½ minutes, led by as many as 31 points in the second half and set a school record for free-throw attempts with 59, hitting 41.

But on December 21 came news that Osborne and Sanders also would be ineligible for the second semester. The blow couldn't have come at a worse time — two days before the Cards would meet revenge-minded, fourth-ranked UK (6-1) in Rupp Arena.

And the Wildcats, who would be crowned national champions three months later, extended the nightmare by thrashing the Cards, 89-66, behind a 30-point performance by guard Tony Delk.

"They just physically dominated us," Crum said.

U of L bounced back to win nine of its next 11 games, including its Conference USA debut at Saint Louis (67-63) and a rare win at DePaul (81-71). There were two extraordinary performances by the short-handed Cards during the streak — against UCLA and Memphis.

Two games after Walker was declared ineligible indefinitely, U of L headed west without its star center for what figured to be a public execution. Instead, the Cards pulled off one of their biggest shockers ever, jarring No. 15 UCLA, 78-76, on Brian Kiser's three-pointer with four seconds left to give Crum his first victory at Pauley in eight tries.

The Cards, who forced the Bruins into 25 turnovers, trailed by 14 points late in the first half, then led by 13 with 13:30 left in the game. "But we knew they'd come back," said Wheat, who was spectacular in collecting 25 points, nine assists, five steals, and five rebounds.

They did, reclaiming the lead at 76-75 on a steal and dunk by Charles O'Bannon at 0:35. Crum called time-out to set up a shot for either Wheat or Kiser, who had been red-hot all day. Kiser came off Damion Dantzler's screen on the right wing and nailed the game-winning three — his sixth of the game in eight attempts — for a career-high 20 points.

"The first thing I thought was 'Praise God,' " said Kiser, a born-again Christian. "Then, 'Play defense.' "

"We were outmanned in every area you can think of," said Wheat, whose four threes gave him 200 for his career. "It was just heart."

A week later the victim was No. 11 Conference USA rival Memphis, 74-56, in Freedom Hall. The win and the margin weren't the only surprises of the evening. There was junior center Beau Zach Smith's inspired performance against Player of the Year candidate Lorenzen Wright, Kiser's career-best nine rebounds to go along with a team-high 18 points and a suffocating defense that held the Tigers to a season-low 26.7 percent shooting.

The streak ended with a 68-65 home loss to Tulane, but the Cards won three more in a row, capped by the sterling 72-66 upset of No. 6 Cincinnati, which had won 13 straight at home. Incredibly, U of L won even though it committed 26 turnovers, shot only 41.3 percent

RETIREMENT NOT IN THE CARDS

Denny Crum's contract calls for him to coach the University of Louisville basketball team through 1997-98, which would make him 61 years old and mark 27 years with the Cardinals. Will he retire then or coach longer? Crum insists he hasn't decided. But if he were to step down, he would have no trouble finding something to occupy his time because he loves to hunt, fish, and play golf.

However he also loves to coach, and basketball has been his life since his days as a guard on the San Fernando High School team in Los Angeles. He has coached on the college level for 38 years.

Crum has the same response to questions about possible retirement as he's always had:

"I'm going to coach for as long as they want me or until I get tired of it. I don't know when that will be. All I know is that when fall rolls around and I'm not ready to go to practice, I'll give it up. I wish I knew when that will happen; it would make life a lot easier to plan.

"I still love teaching and coaching and the challenge of young people. I love the competition. It's all part of me; it's what I do and it's what I've always done."

When Crum quits coaching, he'll still be active, whether it's fishing for trout or salmon in Alaska, bass fishing on a lake in Kentucky, hunting (he has bagged a brown bear, among other trophies) or winning bets from friends on the golf course.

"When I get to the point I'm not active anymore, I won't have any problem finding things to do," he said. "I'm too active and there are too many things I like, so I certainly won't get bored."

But John Wooden, for one, doesn't expect Crum to retire soon. "I'll be surprised if he stops before 65," Wooden said.

(Wheat was zero for nine), and three players fouled out.

"We're 6-0 in conference play on the road, and I don't know how," Crum said. "I wish I could give you the exact formula and sell it. These kids just don't want to quit. They keep hustling, and they get it done."

But they couldn't quite get it done in the next three games, losing by a total of seven points at Memphis (57-54) and at home to Marquette (80-79 in double overtime) and No. 2 UMass (62-59). At Memphis, Wheat continued to be bothered by a jammed finger on his shooting hand and extended a shooting slump by hitting just two of 16.

Against Marquette on February 28 Walker played for the first time since January 17. He got 24 points and 12 rebounds, but Aaron Hutchins hit a three-pointer with three seconds left in the second OT to lift the Eagles to victory. U of L's loss to UMass also wasn't decided until the final seconds, when Wheat's three-pointer at 0:02

Although he played only two seasons, 6-9 center Samaki Walker recorded the only triple-double in U of L history. He collected 14 points, 10 rebounds and 11 blocks in the Cards' 88-86 upset of sixth-ranked Kentucky as a freshman in 1995. He turned pro following the '95-96 season and was a first-round pick of the Dallas Mavericks.

was partially blocked.

That sent the Cards into the Conference USA Tournament in Memphis on a three-game losing skid. They buried Tulane, 98-79, shooting 60.4 percent, outrebounding the bigger opponent 43-28, and getting 23 points and seven rebounds from Sims, to set up a semifinal rematch with top-seeded Cincinnati. This time the Bearcats built a 19-point lead while rolling to a 92-81 victory.

However, U of L hadn't depleted its bagful of surprises quite yet. Seeded No. 6 in the Midwest Regional in Milwaukee, the Cards rallied from a 12-point deficit in the final 3:40 to oust Tulsa, 82-80, in overtime, then upset third-seeded Villanova, 68-64.

A welcome sight against Tulsa was Wheat's returning to his former self, scoring 33 points on 10-of-18 shooting to help overcome an 0-for-9 performance by the starting front line.

U of L's defense ignited the comeback against Tulsa, which committed 28 turnovers. The Cards had 18 steals, with Wheat getting five, Rogers four, and Kiser and Sims three apiece. And Flynn provided his usual spark off the bench, with 11 points. Walker sent the game into overtime with a dunk off a pass from Kiser, completing a 13-1 run, and Wheat's three at 0:47.8 in OT gave U of L the lead for good at 78-77.

It was more of Wheat against No. 10 Villanova. Wheat, whose three gave U of L a 49-36 lead with 13:32 left and whose two free throws at 0:15.1 iced it, finished with a team-high 19 points and three assists as the Cards beat a higher-seeded team for the first time since 1988.

"Coming in, I don't think Villanova thought we could beat them," said Rogers. "But who did? Ask anybody. But we believe in ourselves. What we did today is what we've done all year. We're always beating teams that nobody gave us a chance to beat."

The Cards nearly did it once more, but they fell one-point short the following week in the Midwest semis in Minneapolis against second-seeded and ninth-ranked Wake Forest and its All-America center Tim Duncan.

Wheat's potential game-winning 10-footer with four seconds left bounced off the rim. After averaging 26 points in the first two tournament games, Wheat went three-for-15, and U of L hit only 33.3 percent.

"How many times have I made a shot like that?" Wheat asked in reference to his last shot. "A lot of times. I've missed a few, but I've made more than I've missed. Unfortunately, this one just didn't go in."

Thus the Magical Mystery Tour ended. But what a ride it was!

CARDINALS QUIZ

37. True or false. The 1944-45 squad is the only U of L team to defeat every team it played at least once.

CARDINALS QUIZ

38. When was the first time U of L scored more than 100 points during a game?

By the Numbers

The statistics, lists and records that appear in this chapter are taken from the U of L basketball media guide, which is produced by the U of L Sports Information Office. The text was updated through the 1995-96 season.

SEASON-BY-SEASON SUMMARY

Year	Coach	Won	Lost	Pct	Post-Season Tournament
1911-12	William Gardiner	0	3	.000	—
1912-13	Captains	2	3	.400	—
1913-14	Captains	2	6	.250	—
1914-15	Captains	4	5	.444	—
1915-16	Ed Bowman	8	3	.727	—
1916-17	No Formal Team				
1917-18	Ed Bowman	3	4	.429	—
1918-19	Earl Ford	7	4	.636	—
1919-20	Tuley Brucker	6	5	.545	—
1920-21	Jimmie Powers	3	6	.273	—
1921-22	Dr. John T. O'Rouke	1	13	.071	—
1922-23	No Formal Team				
1923-24	Fred Enke	4	13	.235	—
1924-25	Fred Enke	10	7	.588	—
1925-26	Tom King	4	8	.333	KIAC
1926-27	Tom King	7	5	.583	KIAC
1927-28	Tom King	12	4	.750	KIAC
1928-29	Tom King	12	8	.600	KIAC
1929-30	Tom King	9	6	.600	KIAC & SIAA
1930-31	Edward Weber	5	11	.313	KIAC
1931-32	Edward Weber	15	7	.682	KIAC & SIAA
1932-33	C.V. Money	11	11	.500	KIAC
1933-34	C.V. Money	16	9	.640	KIAC & SIAA
1934-35	C.V. Money	5	9	.357	KIAC
1935-36	C.V. Money	14	11	.560	KIAC & SIAA
1936-37	Lawrence Apitz	4	8	.333	KIAC
1937-38	Lawrence Apitz	4	11	.267	KIAC
1938-39	Lawrence Apitz	1	15	.063	KIAC
1939-40	Lawrence Apitz	1	18	.053	KIAC
1940-41	John C. Heldman, Jr.	2	14	.125	KIAC
1941-42	John C. Heldman, Jr.	7	10	.412	KIAC
1942-43	No Formal Team				
1943-44	Harold Church & Walter Casey	10	10	.500	—
1944-45	Bernard Hickman	16	3	.842	—
1945-46	Bernard Hickman	22	6	.786	KIAC
1946-47	Bernard Hickman	17	6	.739	KIAC
1947-48	Bernard Hickman	29	6	.829	KIAC, NAIB & Olympic Trials
1948-49	Bernard Hickman	23	10	.697	OVC
1949-50	Bernard Hickman	21	11	.656	—
1950-51	Bernard Hickman	19	7	.731	NCAA
1951-52	Bernard Hickman	20	6	.769	NIT
1952-53	Bernard Hickman	22	6	.786	NIT
1953-54	Bernard Hickman	22	7	.759	NIT
1954-55	Bernard Hickman	19	8	.704	NIT
1955-56	Bernard Hickman	26	3	.897	NIT
1956-57	Bernard Hickman	21	5	.808	—
1957-58	Bernard Hickman	13	12	.520	—
1958-59	Bernard Hickman	19	12	.613	NCAA
1959-60	Bernard Hickman	15	11	.577	—
1960-61	Bernard Hickman	21	8	.724	NCAA
1961-62	Bernard Hickman	15	10	.600	—
1962-63	Bernard Hickman	14	11	.560	—
1963-64	Bernard Hickman	15	10	.600	NCAA
1964-65	Bernard Hickman	15	10	.600	—
1965-66	Bernard Hickman	16	10	.615	NIT
1966-67	Bernard Hickman	23	5	.821	NCAA

Year	Coach	Won	Lost	Pct	Post-Season Tournament
1967-68	John Dromo	21	7	.750	NCAA
1968-69	John Dromo	21	6	.778	NIT
1969-70	John Dromo	18	9	.667	NIT
1970-71	John Dromo, Howard Stacey	20	9	.689	NIT
1971-72	Denny Crum	26	5	.839	NCAA
1972-73	Denny Crum	23	7	.767	NIT
1973-74	Denny Crum	21	7	.750	NCAA
1974-75	Denny Crum	28	3	.903	NCAA
1975-76	Denny Crum	20	8	.714	NIT
1976-77	Denny Crum	21	7	.750	NCAA
1977-78	Denny Crum	23	7	.767	NCAA
1978-79	Denny Crum	24	8	.750	NCAA
1979-80	Denny Crum	33	3	.917	NCAA
1980-81	Denny Crum	21	9	.700	NCAA
1981-82	Denny Crum	23	10	.697	NCAA
1982-83	Denny Crum	32	4	.889	NCAA
1983-84	Denny Crum	24	11	.686	NCAA
1984-85	Denny Crum	19	18	.514	NIT
1985-86	Denny Crum	32	7	.821	NCAA
1986-87	Denny Crum	18	14	.563	—
1987-88	Denny Crum	24	11	.686	NCAA
1988-89	Denny Crum	24	9	.727	NCAA
1989-90	Denny Crum	27	8	.771	NCAA
1990-91	Denny Crum	14	16	.467	----
1991-92	Denny Crum	19	11	.633	NCAA
1992-93	Denny Crum	22	9	.710	NCAA
1993-94	Denny Crum	28	6	.824	NCAA
1994-95	Denny Crum	19	14	.576	NCAA
1995-96	Denny Crum	22	12	.647	NCAA
Totals	**82 Seasons**	**1299**	**687**	**.654**	

COACHING RECORDS

Years	Coach	Yrs.	Won	Lost	Pct.
1911-1912	William Gardiner	1	0	3	.000
1912-1915	Coached by Players	3	8	14	.363
1915-1918	Ed Bowman	2*	11	8	.578
1918-1919	Earl Ford	1**	7	3	.700
1919-1920	Tuley Brucker	1	6	5	.545
1920-1921	Jimmie Powers	1	3	8	.272
1921-1922	Dr. John T. O'Rourke	1	1	13	.071
1922-1923	No Formal Team				
1923-1925	Fred Enke, Sr.	2	14	20	.411
1925-1930	Tom King	5	44	31	.586
1930-1932	Eddie Weber	2	20	18	.526
1932-1936	C.V. (Red) Money	4	46	40	.534
1936-1940	Lawrence E. (Laurie) Apitz	4	10	52	.161
1940-1942	John C. Heldman, Jr.	2	9	24	.272
1942-1943	No Formal Team				
1943-1944	C.Spec. Harold Church and C.Spec. Walter Casey	1	10	10	.500
1944-1967	Bernard L. (Peck) Hickman	23	443	183	.708
1967-1971	John Dromo	4***	68	23	.747
1970-1971	Howard Stacey	1****	12	8	.600
1971-present	Denny Crum	25	587	224	.724
Totals		**82**	**1299**	**687**	**.654**

* There was no formal team in 1916-17. Also, Bowman coached the opening season loss in 1918-19, then turned the team over to Earl Ford.
** Earl Ford was named head coach after the 1918-19 season opener.
*** John Dromo suffered a heart attack after nine games in 1970-71 and did not complete his fourth season.
**** Assistant Coach Howard Stacey was named interim head coach on Jan. 3, 1971, following John Dromo's heart attack. Stacey served as U of L's head coach for the final 20 games of the 1970-71 season.

INDIVIDUAL RECORDS

POINTS, GAME

Overall — 45, Wes Unseld vs. Georgetown (Col.), Dec. 1, 1967
Overall half — 26, Charlie Tyra vs. Notre Dame, Dec. 22, 1956; Butch Beard vs. Bradley, Jan. 14, 1967
Home Court — 45, Wes Unseld vs. Georgetown(Col.), Dec. 1, 1967
Opponent's Court — 44, Bud Olsen vs. Ky. Wesleyan, Mar. 3, 1962
First Half — 21, Junior Bridgeman vs. Rutgers, Mar. 15, 1975; Everick Sullivan vs. Chaminade, Nov. 24, 1989
Second Half — 26, Butch Beard vs Bradley, Jan. 14, 1967
Losing Effort — 36, Wes Unseld vs. Northwestern, Dec. 9, 1967
By opponent, Game — 47, Joel Curbelo, American (Puerto Rico), Nov. 24, 1995
By opponent, Half — 27, Jerry West, West Virginia, Mar. 20, 1959; 27, Joel Curbelo, American (Puerto Rico), Nov. 24, 1995

POINTS, SEASON

Overall — 825, Darrell Griffith, 1979-80 (36 games)
Average — 23.8, Charlie Tyra, 1955-56 (29 games)
    Freshman — 14.1, Wesley Cox, 1973-74
    Sophomore — 20.5, Butch Beard, 1966-67
    Junior — 23.8, Charlie Tyra, 1955-56
    Senior — 23.1, John Turner, 1960-61

POINTS, CAREER

Overall — 2,333, Darrell Griffith, 1976-80 (126 games)
Average — 20.6, Wes Unseld, 1965-68 (1,686 in 82 games)

FIELD GOALS, GAME

Made game — 20, Butch Beard vs. Bradley, Jan. 14, 1967
Made by opponent game — 19, Bill Ebben (Detroit), Mar. 6, 1957
Made half — 13, Butch Beard vs. Bradley, Jan. 14, 1967
Made by opponent half — 11, Larry Hennessey (Villanova), Dec. 16, 1950; Bobby Smith (Tulsa), Feb. 13, 1969; Rick Whitlow (Illinois State), Mar. 4, 1974
Attempted — 33, John Reuther vs. DePaul, Feb. 26, 1964
Attempted by opponent — 42, Dwight Lamar (SW Louisiana) Mar. 16,1972
Consecutive Made — 19, Clifford Rozier (made last 2 vs. Morehead St., Dec. 8, 1993; all 15 vs. Eastern Ky., Dec. 11, 1993; first 2 vs. Wyoming, Dec. 18, 1993)
Percentage (min. of 10 att.) — 1.000, Clifford Rozier vs. Eastern Ky., Dec. 11, 1993 (15-15); Cornelius Holden vs. Southern Miss., Mar. 3, 1990 (14-14); Derek Smith vs. Marquette, Feb. 14, 1981 (12-12); Troy Smith vs. Tulane, Feb. 27, 1993

FIELD GOALS, SEASON

Made — 349, Darrell Griffith, 1979-80 (36 games)
Attempted — 631, Darrell Griffith, 1979-80 (36 games)
Percentage — .681, Felton Spencer, 1989-90 (188-276) (min. 130 attempts)

FIELD GOALS, CAREER

Made — 981, Darrell Griffith (4 years), 1976-80 (126 games); 632, Darrell Griffith (3 years), 1976-79 (90 games)
Attempted — 1877, Darrell Griffith (4 yrs), 1976-80 (126 games); 1430, John Turner (3 yrs), 1958-61 (86 games)
Percentage — .628, Felton Spencer (409-651), 1986-90 (min. 325 attempts)

FREE THROWS, GAME

Made — 16, Charlie Tyra vs. Notre Dame, Dec. 22, 1956
Made half — 14, LaBradford Smith vs. Indiana, Dec. 19, 1987
Made by opponent-game — 21, Jack Adams (Eastern Ky.), Feb. 9, 1955
By opponent-half — 14, Jack Adams (Eastern Kentucky), Feb. 9, 1955; Bill Haig (DePaul), Feb. 17, 1959
Attempted — 26, Clarence Rodgers vs. Moore's Hill, Feb. 28, 1913
By opponent — 28, Jack Adams (Eastern Kentucky), Feb. 9, 1955
Consecutive Made — 14, LaBradford Smith vs. Indiana, Dec. 19, 1987

FREE THROWS, SEASON

Made — 177, Wes Unseld, 1967-68 (28 games)
Attempted — 275, Wes Unseld, 1967-68 (28 games)
Consecutive Made — 36, LaBradford Smith, 1987-88
Percentage — .905, LaBradford Smith, 1987-88, (143-158) (min. 50 attempts)

FREE THROWS, CAREER

Made — 491, LaBradford Smith (4 years), 1987-91 (133 games) 426, Wes Unseld (3 years), 1965-68 (82 games)
Attempted — 686, Charlie Tyra (4 years), 1953-57 (95 games) 654, Wes Unseld (3 years), 1965-68 (82 games)
Percentage (min. 135 attempts) — .866, LaBradford Smith, 1987-91 (491-567)

MINUTES PLAYED (NUMBER)

Season — 1,312, Milt Wagner, 1985-86
Career — 4,335, Pervis Ellison, 1985-89

REBOUNDS, GAME

Made — 38, Charlie Tyra vs. Canisius, Dec. 10, 1955
Made by opponent — 30, Wendell Ladner (Southern Miss.), Dec. 7, 1968

REBOUNDS, SEASON

Overall — 645, Charlie Tyra, 1955-56 (29 games)
Average — 22.2, Charlie Tyra, 1955-56 (645 in 29 games)

REBOUNDS, CAREER

Overall — 1,617, Charlie Tyra (4 years), 1953-57 (95 games); 1,551, Wes Unseld (3 years), 1965-68 (82 games)
Average — 18.9, Wes Unseld, 1965-68 (1,551 in 29 games)

THREE-POINT GOALS, GAME

Made — 8 (in 14 att.), James Brewer vs. Oral Roberts, Jan.2, 1993
Percentage: 1.000, Everick Sullivan (6-6) vs. Virginia, Feb. 17, 1990

THREE-POINT GOALS, SEASON

Made — 84, DeJuan Wheat, 1994-95 (84-195)
Percentage (min. 100 attempts) — .458, Brian Kiser, 1994-95 (55-120)

THREE-POINT GOALS, CAREER

Made: 226, DeJuan Wheat, 1993-96 (226-584)
Percentage (min. 150 attempts) — .461, Dwayne Morton (111-241), 1991-94

FOULS COMMITTED

Season — 130, Dick Robinson, 1949-50
Career — 414, Pervis Ellison, 1985-89

ASSISTS

Game — 14, Phil Bond vs. UCLA, March 12, 1977
Game, Made by opponent — 15, Jim Les (Cleveland State), Feb. 25, 1982
Season — 226, LaBradford Smith, 1989-90 (35 games)
Career — 713, LaBradford Smith, 1987-90 (133 games)

GAMES, SEASON

Appeared In — 39, Milt Wagner, Billy Thompson, Jeff Hall, Herbert Crook, Pervis Ellison, and Tony Kimbro; all in 1985-86

GAMES, CAREER

Appeared In — 145, Jeff Hall, 1982-86
Games Started — 135, Pervis Ellison, 1985-89
Consecutive Starts — 133, LaBradford Smith, 1987-91

STEALS

Game — 10, Tick Rogers vs. Western Carolina, Dec. 5, 1994
Season — 86, Darrell Griffith, 1979-80; Tick Rogers, 1994-95
Career — 230, Darrell Griffith, 1976-80

BLOCKED SHOTS

Game — 11, Samaki Walker vs. Kentucky, Jan. 1, 1995
Season — 102, Pervis Ellison, 1987-88
Career — 374, Pervis Ellison, 1985-89

DUNKS

Game — 7, Pervis Ellison vs. South Alabama, Jan. 4, 1988
Season — 59, Pervis Ellison, 1987-88
Career — 162, Pervis Ellison, 1985-89

TEAM RECORDS

POINTS, GAME

Overall — 132, vs. George Mason, Jan. 4, 1994
Overall half — 70, vs. Memphis State, Feb. 25, 1978
By opponent — 107, Illinois State, Mar. 4, 1974
By opponent, half — 61, Wichita State, Feb. 16, 1966
Most made by both teams — 224, vs. Illinois State, Mar. 4, 1974 (L-117, ISU-107)
Losing Effort — 98, vs. Oklahoma, Mar. 24, 1988, NCAA Southeast Regional, Birmingham, Alabama
Home Court — 132, vs. George Mason, Jan. 4, 1994
Neutral Court — 126, vs. St. Peter's, Dec. 28, 1971, New York, Holiday Festival Tournament
Opponent Court — 116, vs. Kentucky Wesleyan, Feb. 4, 1956

POINTS, SEASON

Louisville — 3,096, 1985-86 (39 games)
Opponents — 2,694, 1985-86 (39 games)
Average — 86.0, 1955-56 (2,494 in 29 games)
By opponent — 77.9, 1973-74 (2,183 in 28 games)

FIELD GOALS, GAME

Overall Game — 51, vs. Tampa, Feb. 3, 1962
Overall Half — 27, vs. Tampa, Feb. 3, 1962; vs. Xavier, Feb. 12, 1964
Opponent game — 44, Illinois State, Mar. 4, 1964
Opponent half — 24, Oral Roberts, Mar. 14, 1974
Attempted game — 126, vs. Hanover, Dec. 11, 1946 (made 25)
Attempted by opponent — 106, Illinois State, Mar. 4, 1974 (made 44)
By both teams — 199, vs. LSU, Dec. 22, 1949 (LSU 102-L 97)
Percentage half — .815 vs. Kentucky, Mar. 26, 1983 (22-27)
Percentage game — .714 vs. Marquette, Feb. 14, 1981 (30-42); vs. Duke, Jan. 12, 1983 (40-56)
Percentage opponent — .673, North Carolina State , Feb. 13, 1988 (35-52)
Lowest percentage — .122, Kentucky Wesleyan, Feb. 7, 1929 (9-74)
Lowest percentage by opponent — .145 Georgetown (Col.), Dec. 2, 1955 (10-69)

FIELD GOALS, SEASON

Most made — 1,212, 1985-86 (39 games)
By opponents — 1,067, 1985-86 (39 games)
Attempted — 2,378, 1973-74 (28 games)
By opponents — 2,245, 1989-90 (35 games)
Best percentage — .531, 1985-86 (1,212 - 2,281)
Opponents — .457, 1985-86 (1,067 - 2,336)

FREE THROWS, GAME

Made — 44, vs. Canisius, Dec. 10, 1955
Opponent — 44, by Siena, Dec. 10, 1953
Half — 31, vs. Virginia Tech, Feb. 10, 1986
Half by opponent — 24, by Cincinnati, Jan. 11, 1969
Attempted — 59, vs. Texas, Dec. 9, 1995 (made 41)
Attempted by both teams — 110, Siena, Dec. 10, 1953 (S-68, L-52)
Percentage — 1.000, vs. New Mexico State, Jan. 30, 1975 (19 - 19)
Percentage by opponent — 1.000, Wichita State, Mar. 3, 1965 (19 - 19); Eastern Kentucky, Jan. 6, 1986 (5 - 5)
Lowest percentage — .182, vs. Eastern Kentucky, Jan. 17, 1930 (2 - 11)
By opponent — .111, Rose Poly, Jan. 12, 1924 (2 - 18)
Consecutive game — 28, vs. Indiana, Dec. 19, 1987
Opponent — 18, Marquette, Jan. 1, 1964 Wichita State, Mar. 3, 1965

FREE THROWS, SEASON

Made — 672, 1985-86 (39 games)
Opponent — 735, 1953-54 (29 games)
Attempted — 1,098, 1953-54, (29 games)
Percentage — .752, 1974-75 (543-722)
Opponent's Pct. — .750, 1950-51 (470-627)
Most consecutive season — 30, 1975-76 (First 6 vs. Bradley Jan. 25, 1975; 19-19 vs. New Mexico State Jan. 30,
    1975; Last 5 vs. North Texas State Feb. 1, 1975)

GAMES

Regular Season — 32, 1949-50
With Post-Season — 39, 1985-86

REBOUNDS, GAME

Made — 74, vs. Arizona, Dec. 27, 1955; vs. Tampa, Dec. 13, 1966; vs. St. Peter's, Dec. 28, 1971
Made by opponent — 103, Xavier, Jan. 4, 1958
Both teams — 172, vs. Xavier, Jan. 4, 1958 (X-103, L-69)

REBOUNDS, SEASON

Most — 1,696, 1958-59 (31 games)
By opponent — 1,570, 1958-59 (31 games)
Average — 55.6, 1955-56 (1,611 in 29 games)
By opponent — 52.2, 1959-60 (1,357 in 26 games)

THREE-POINT GOALS

Game — 16 (in 30 attempts) vs. Oral Roberts, Jan. 2, 1993
Season — 229 (in 627 attempts), 1994-95 (33 games)

FOULS, GAME

Most — 43, vs. Siena, Dec. 10, 1953
By opponent — 38, Cincinnati, Mar. 8, 1986; Texas, Dec. 9, 1995
Both teams — 73, vs. Siena, Dec. 10, 1953 (L-43, S-30)
Most fouled out — 6, vs. Denver, Feb. 8, 1950 (41 fouls)
By opponent — 6, Eastern Kentucky, Feb. 18, 1953 (37 fouls); Virginia Tech, Feb. 10, 1986 (35 fouls)
Fouled out, both teams — 8, vs. Denver, Feb. 8, 1950 (L-6, D-2); vs. Eastern Kentucky, Feb. 18, 1953 (EKU-6, L-2)

FOULS, SEASON

Most — 756, 1949-50 (32 games)
By opponent — 802, 1985-86 (39 games)

ASSISTS, GAME

Made — 32, vs. Syracuse, Mar. 31, 1975; vs. Bradley, Mar. 1, 1976; vs. Kentucky, Dec. 26, 1975; vs. Dayton,
     Jan. 26, 1988
By opponent — 29, Tulsa, Jan. 4, 1969; North Carolina State, Feb. 13, 1988

ASSISTS, SEASON

Made — 661, 1989-90
By opponent — 528, 1987-88

TURNOVERS, GAME

Made — 38, vs. Hawaii-Hilo, Dec. 20, 1984
By opponent — 39, Bellarmine, Mar. 4, 1968

BLOCKED SHOTS

Game — 17, vs. Kentucky, Jan. 1, 1995
Season — 251, 1982-83

STEALS

Game — 21, vs. Tulsa, Feb. 22, 1975
Season — 335, 1994-95

DUNKS

Game — 12 vs. Virginia Tech, Feb. 2, 1990
Season — 195, 1989-90

MISCELLANEOUS RECORDS

GAME

Margin of victory — 72, vs Georgetown (Col.), Dec. 2, 1944 (L-99, G-27)
Margin by opponent — 54, Centre, 1920 (C-61, L-7)
Most overtimes — 3, vs. Xavier, Jan. 4, 1958 (X-82, L-80); vs. DePaul, Feb. 7, 1962 (D-79, L-78); vs.
     Cincinnati, Jan. 19, 1965 (L-82, C-80); vs. Boston College, Mar. 12, 1966 (BC-96, L-90)

SEASON

Most wins — 33, 1979-80 (33-3)
Win streak — 18, During the 1979-80 NCAA title winning year, U of L had a 7-2 record when the 18-game
     streak started, a 65-68 win over Nebraska in the Hawaii Rainbow Classic, on Dec. 30, 1979. The
     streak ended on Feb. 21, 1980 in Madison Square Garden when Iona beat Louisville by a 77-60 score.
     The loss was the team's third and final loss of the season.
Most consecutive winning seasons — 46, Beginning with a 16-3 record in 1944-45 and continuing through
     1989-90 when Louisville was 27-8.
Most losses — 18, 1939-40 (1-18)1984-85 (19-18)
Losing streak — 19, Last two games of 1938-39, starting with a 50-27 loss to Georgetown College on Feb. 18,
     1939, and the first 17 games of 1939-40, ending with a 56-55 victory over Berea on Feb. 22, 1940
Fewest victories — 0, 1911-12 (0-3)
Fewest losses — 3, (on seven occasions; last - 1979-80)
Highest won-lost percentage — .917, 1979-80 (33-3)
Lowest won-lost percentage — .000, 1911-12 (0-3)
Longest shot made — 70 feet, Marv Selvy vs. Wichita State, Feb. 24, 1968
Longest shot made, opponent — 60 feet, Warren Armstrong (Wichita State), Feb. 10, 1968
Most consecutive games scoring in double figures — 57, Allen Murphy, beginning Jan. 29, 1973 through Feb.
     1, 1975

ATTENDANCE RECORDS

One Game, Away — 61,612, vs. Georgetown, Mar. 27, 1982 at New Orleans Superdome
One Game, Home — 19,872 vs. UCLA, March 5, 1995
Season Total — 603,086, 1988-89 33 games (18,275 average); 587,076, 1985-86 39 games (15,053 average);
     554,950, 1987-88 35 games (15,856 average)
Season Home — 346,782, 1985-86 18 games (19,265 average); 343,572, 1984-85 19 games (18,082 average)

DENNY CRUM'S RECORDS

YEAR-BY-YEAR RECORD

Year	Home	Away	Overall	Pct.	Conference	Pct.
1971-72	11-1	15-4	26-5	.838	12-2	.857
1972-73	14-1	9-6	23-7	.766	11-3	.786
1973-74	12-2	9-5	21-7	.750	11-1	.917
1974-75	14-0	14-3	28-3	.903	12-2	.857
1975-76	13-4	7-4	20-8	.714	—	—
1976-77	15-1	6-6	21-7	.750	6-1	.857
1977-78	13-2	10-5	23-7	.766	9-3	.750
1978-79	15-1	9-7	24-8	.750	9-1	.900
1979-80	16-0	17-3	33-3	.917	12-0	1.000
1980-81	14-2	7-7	21-9	.700	11-1	.917
1981-82	11-2	12-8	23-10	.697	8-4	.667
1982-83	14-1	18-3	32-4	.889	12-0	1.000
1983-84	13-2	11-9	24-11	.686	11-3	.786
1984-85	14-5	5-13	19-18	.514	6-8	.429
1985-86	17-1	15-6	32-7	.825	10-2	.833
1986-87	12-5	6-9	18-14	.563	9-3	.750
1987-88	14-2	10-9	24-11	.686	11-3	.786
1988-89	11-4	13-5	24-9	.727	8-4	.667
1989-90	12-2	15-6	27-8	.771	12-2	.857
1990-91	9-6	5-10	14-16	.467	4-10	.286
1991-92	11-4	8-7	19-11	.633	7-5	.583
1992-93	13-3	9-6	22-9	.710	11-1	.917
1993-94	14-1	14-5	28-6	.824	10-2	.833
1994-95	14-3	5-11	19-14	.576	7-5	.583
1995-96	10-4	12-8	22-12	.647	10-4	.714
Totals	326-59	261-164	587-224	.724	229-70	.766

COACHING HONORS

1973	Missouri Valley Conf. Co-Coach of Year
1974	Kentucky Sports World Coach of Year
1979	Metro Conference Coach of the Year
1980	Basketball Weekly Coach of the Year
1980	Metro Conference Coach of the Year
1983	The Sporting News Coach of the Year
1983	Metro Conference Coach of the Year
1986	The Sporting News Coach of the Year
1986	Playboy Coach of the Year
1986	Basketball Weekly Man of the Year
1986	Lexington Herald-Leader Sportsman of the Year
1990	Lexington Herald-Leader Sportsman of the Decade
1994	Naismith Memorial Basketball Hall of Fame
1994	Metro Conference Coach of the Year
1994	Kodak/NABC District III Coach of the Year
1996	Conference USA Coach of the Year

WINNINGEST DIVISION I MEN'S COACHES

ACTIVE COACHES, BY PERCENTAGE

(Minimum five years as a Division I head coach; includes record at four-year colleges only).

	Coach, College	Yrs.	Won	Lost	Pct.
1.	Jerry Tarkanian, Fresno	25	647	133	.829
2.	Roy Williams, Kansas	8	213	56	.792
3.	John Kresse, Charleston (S.C.)	17	412	109	.791
4.	Dean Smith, N. Carolina	35	851	247	.775
5.	Jim Boeheim, Syracuse	20	483	159	.752
6.	Nolan Richardson, Ark.	16	391	132	.748
7.	Bill Herrion, Drexel	5	112	38	.747
8.	John Chaney, Temple	24	540	188	.742
9.	Bob Knight, Indiana	31	678	247	.733
10.	Larry Hunter, Ohio	20	430	159	.730
11.	Bill Musselman, S. Ala.	11	209	78	.728
12.	Rick Pitino, Kentucky	14	317	119	.727
13.	John Thompson, Georgetown	24	553	208	.727
14.	Denny Crum, Louisville	24	587	224	.724
15.	Lute Olson, Arizona	23	507	194	.723

ACTIVE COACHES, BY VICTORIES

(Minimum five years as a Division I head coach; includes record at four-year colleges only).

	Coach, College	Years	Wins
1.	Dean Smith, North Carolina	35	851
2.	James Phelan, Mt. St. Mary's (Md.)	42	758
3.	Bob Knight, Indiana	31	678
	Don Haskins, UTEP	35	678
	Norm Stewart, Missouri	35	678
6.	Lefty Driesell, James Madison	34	667
7.	Jerry Tarkanian, Fresno State	25	647
8.	Denny Crum, Louisville	25	587
9.	Eddie Sutton, Oklahoma State	26	570
10.	John Thompson, Georgetown	24	553

ALL-TIME COACHES, BY PERCENTAGE

(Minimum 10 head coaching seasons in Division I)

	Coach	Yrs.	Won	Lost	Pct.
1.	Jerry Tarkanian, Fresno	25	647	133	.829
2.	Clair Bee, LIU, Brooklyn	21	412	87	.826
3.	Adolph Rupp, Kentucky	41	876	190	.822
4.	John Wooden, UCLA	29	664	162	.804
5.	Dean Smith, N. Carolina	35	851	247	.775
6.	Harry Fisher, Army	13	147	44	.770
7.	Frank Keaney, Rh. Island	27	387	117	.768
8.	George Keogan, N. Dame	24	385	117	.767
9.	Jack Ramsay, St. Joe's	11	231	71	.765
10.	Vic Bubas, Duke	10	213	67	.761
11.	Jim Boeheim, Syracuse	20	483	159	.752
12.	Charles Davies,Duquesne	21	314	106	.748
13.	Nolan Richardson, Ark.	16	391	132	.748
14.	Ray Mears, Tennessee	21	399	135	.747
15.	John Chaney, Temple	24	540	188	.742
16.	Al McGuire, Marquette	20	405	143	.739
17.	Everett Case, N. Car. St.	18	376	133	.739
18.	F.C. "Phog" Allen, Kan.	48	746	264	.739
19.	Walter Meanwell, Mo.	22	280	101	.735
20.	Bob Knight, Indiana	31	678	247	.733
21.	Rick Pitino, Kentucky	14	317	119	.727
22.	John Thompson, G-town	24	553	208	.727
23.	Lew Andreas, Syracuse	25	355	134	.726
24.	Lou Carnesecca, St. John	24	526	200	.725
25.	Denny Crum, Louisville	25	587	224	.724

ALL-TIME COACHES, BY VICTORIES

(Minimum 10 head coaching seasons in Division I)

	Coach, College	Yrs	Wins
1.	Adolph Rupp , Kentucky	41	876
2.	Dean Smith, North Carolina	35	851
3.	Henry Iba, NW Mo. St., Col, Okla. St.	41	767
4.	Ed Diddle, Western Ky.	42	759
5.	Phog Allen, Baker, Cen. Mo., Kan.	48	746
6.	Ray Meyer, DePaul	42	724
7.	Bob Knight , Army, Indiana	31	678
	Norm Stewart, N. Iowa, Missouri	35	678
	Don Haskins, UTEP	35	678
10.	Lefty Driesell, Davidson, Maryland, James Madison	34	667
11.	John Wooden, Indiana St., UCLA	29	664
12.	Lou Henson, H.-Simmons, New Mex. St., Illinois	34	663
13.	Ralph Miller, Wich. St., Iowa, Ore. St.	38	657
14.	Marv Harshman, Pacific Lutheran, Washington St., Wahington	40	654
15.	Jerry Tarkanian, L. Beach St., UNLV, Fresno State	25	647
16.	Gene Bartow, Central Mo. St., Valparaiso, Mem. St., Illinois, UCLA, Ala.-Birm.	34	647
17.	Cam Henderson, Marshall	35	630
18.	Norm Sloan, Pres., Citadel, North Carolina St., Florida	36	627
19.	Amory "Slats" Gill, Oregon St.	36	599
20.	Abe Lemons, Tex-Pan Am,Okla. City	35	597
21.	Guy Lewis, Houston	30	592
22.	Denny Crum, Louisville	25	587
23.	Eddie Sutton (Creighton, Arkansas, Kentucky, Oklahoma State)	25	570

ALL-TIME NCAA TOURNAMENT COACHING RECORDS

MOST YEARS AT CURRENT SCHOOL

No.	Coach, School (Years)
42	James Phelan, Mt. St. Mary's (Md.)(1955-96)
35	Don Haskins, #UTEP (1962-96)
35	Dean Smith, #North Carolina (1962-96)
29	Norm Stewart, Missouri (1968-96)
25	Denny Crum, #Louisville (1972-96)
25	Bob Knight, Indiana (1972-96)
24	Dale Brown, LSU (1973-96)
24	John Thompson, Georgetown (1973-96)

Has coached only at this school.

MOST TOURNAMENT APPEARANCES

No.	Coach, School (Years)
26	Dean Smith, North Carolina, 1967-95
20	Adolph Rupp, Kentucky, 1942-72
20	Denny Crum, Louisville, 1972-95
20	Bob Knight, Indiana, 1973-95
19	John Thompson, Georgetown, 1975-96
18	Lou Carnesecca, St. John's (N.Y.), 1967-92
18	Lou Henson, New Mexico and Illinois, 1967-95
17	Eddie Sutton, Arkansas, Ky., Okla. St., '74-95
17	Jim Boeheim, Syracuse, 1977-96

MOST CONSEC. TOURN. APPEARANCES

No.	Coach, School (Years)
22	Dean Smith, North Carolina,1975-96
14	John Thompson, Georgetown, 1979-92
11	Eddie Sutton, Arkansas, Kentucky, 1977-87
11	Mike Krzyzewski, Duke, 1984-94
10	Jim Boeheim, Syracuse, 1983-92
10	Dale Brown, Louisiana St., 1984-93
10	Lute Olsen, Arizona, 1985-93
9	Bobby Cremins, Georgia Tech, 1985-93
9	Jerry Tarkanian, Nevada-Las Vegas, 1983-91
9	John Wooden, UCLA, 1967-75
8	Denny Crum, Louisville, 1977-84
8	Billy Tubbs, Oklahoma, 1983-90
8	Lou Henson, Illinois, 1983-90
8	Richard "Digger" Phelps, N. Dame, 1974-81

MOST TOURNAMENT WINS

No.	Coach, School (Years)
61	Dean Smith, North Carolina, 1967-96
47	John Wooden, UCLA, 1950-75
40	Bob Knight, Indiana, 1973-96
39	Denny Crum, Louisville, 1972-96
39	Mike Krzyzewski, Duke, 1984-96
34	John Thompson, Georgetown, 1975-96
31	Jerry Tarkanian, L. Beach St., UNLV, 1970-91
30	Adolph Rupp, Kentucky, 1942-72
27	Eddie Sutton, Arkansas, Ky., Okla. St., '74-96

MOST NCAA CHAMPIONSHIPS

No.	Coach, School (Years)
10	John Wooden, UCLA, 1964-75
4	Adolph Rupp, Kentucky, 1948-58
3	Bob Knight, Indiana, 1976-87
2	Denny Crum, Louisville, 1980-86
2	Mike Krzyzewski, Duke, 1991-92
2	Henry Iba, Oklahoma St., 1945-46
2	Ed Jucker, Cincinnati, 1961-62
2	Branch McCracken, Indiana, 1940-53
2	Dean Smith, North Carolina, 1982-93
2	Phil Woolpert, San Francisco, 1955-56

MOST FINAL FOUR WINS

No.	Coach, School (Years)
21	John Wooden, UCLA, 1962-75
9	Adolph Rupp, Kentucky, 1942-66
8	Dean Smith, North Carolina, 1967-95
7	Bob Knight, Indiana, 1973-92
7	Mike Krzyzewski, Duke, 1986-94
5	Denny Crum, Louisville, 1972-86
5	Henry Iba, Oklahoma St., 1945-51
5	Ed Jucker, Cincinnati, 1961-63
5	Fred Taylor, Ohio St., 1960-68
5	Phil Woolpert, San Francisco, 1955-57

MOST FINAL FOUR APPEARANCES

No.	Coach, School (Years)
12	John Wooden, UCLA, 1962-75
10	Dean Smith, North Carolina, 1967-95
6	Denny Crum, Louisville, 1972-86
6	Mike Krzyzewski, Duke, 1986-94
6	Adolph Rupp, Kentucky, 1942-66
5	Guy Lewis, Houston, 1967-84
5	Bob Knight, Indiana, 1973-92
4	Jack Gardner, Kansas St. and Utah, 1948-66
4	Henry Iba, Oklahoma St., 1945-51
4	Harold Olsen, Ohio St., 1939-46
4	Jerry Tarkanian, Nevada-Las Vegas, 1977-91
4	Fred Taylor, Ohio St., 1960-68

LOUISVILLE ALL-AMERICANS

Season	Player, Team
1955-56	Charlie Tyra, Helms Athletic Foundation
1956-57	Charlie Tyra, Helms Athletic Foundation
1958-59	Don Goldstein, Helms Athletic Foundation
1960-61	John Turner, Helms Athletic Foundation
1965-66	Wes Unseld, Helms Athletic Foundation
1966-67	Wes Unseld, AP, UPI, NABC, Helms, USBWA, Converse
1967-68	Wes Unseld, AP, UPI, NABC, Helms, USBWA, Converse
1968-69	Butch Beard, Helms Athletic Foundation
1971-72	Jim Price, NABC, USBWA, Helms, Converse
1974-75	Junior Bridgeman, NABC, USBWA, Basketball Weekly, Citizens Athletic Foundation, Converse
1974-75	Allen Murphy, Citizens Athletic Foundation
1975-76	Phil Bond, College Sports Information Directors of America (CoSIDA) Academic All-America
1976-77	Wesley Cox, Citizens Athletic Foundation, Converse
1977-78	Rick Wilson, Basketball Weekly
1978-79	Darrell Griffith, Sporting News, Citizens Athletic Foundation, Converse
1979-80	Darrell Griffith, John Wooden Award, Sporting News Player of the Year, Basketball Weekly, Converse, USBWA, AP, UPI, Sport Magazine, Citizens Athletic Foundation; consensus first team
1983-84	Lancaster Gordon, Sporting News (second team)
1988-89	Pervis Ellison, Consensus first team; USBWA and NABC First Teams; AP and UPI Second Teams; Blue Ribbon Yearbook Player of the Year
1993-94	Clifford Rozier, Consensus first team; AP, UPI, USBWA and ESPN Radio first teams; NABC, Basketball Weekly and Basketball Times second teams.

CARDINALS IN THE PROS

Henry Bacon
Louisville (1969-72), San Diego (1972-73)
Played one season with San Diego of the ABA, scoring 166 points in 47 games during the 1972-73 season. Helped the Cardinals reach the NCAA Final Four in 1972, Coach Denny Crum's first season at U of L.

Butch Beard
Louisville (1966-69), Atlanta (1969-70), Cleveland (1971-72,'75-76), Seattle (1972-73), Golden State (1973-75), New York (1975-79)
Tenth pick overall in the 1969 NBA Draft. Played nine seasons in the NBA. Best season as a pro was 1971-72, averaging 15.4 ppg with Cleveland. Scored over 5,571 points in 637 career games.

Phillip Bond
Louisville (1972-77), Houston Rockets (1977-78)
A third round draft pick, Bond played in seven games with the Houston Rockets in the 1977-78 season. Second in career assists at U of L with 528 and two of his single season assist totals are among the top ten for the Cardinals.

Junior Bridgeman
Louisville (1972-75), Milwaukee Bucks (1975-84, 1986-87), L. A. Clippers (1984-86)
Eighth pick in the 1975 draft. Played ten seasons with Milwaukee and two with the Los Angeles Clippers. Averaged double figures in scoring from 1976-85. Finished his NBA career with 11,517 points in 849 games. Had his jersey (No. 2) retired by Milwaukee Bucks.

Roger Burkman
Louisville (1977-81), Chicago Bulls (1981-82)
A sixth round draft pick, Burkman, played briefly one season with the Chicago Bulls. The defensive specialist saw action in six games with Chicago. Known as "Instant Defense" with the Cardinals, helping U of L to the 1980 NCAA title.

Jack Coleman
Louisville (1946-49), Rochester (1949-56), St. Louis (1956-58)
A nine-year veteran of the NBA, playing six and a half years with Rochester and two and a half years with St. Louis. Totalled 6,721 points in 633 career games over his NBA career. Led U of L to the 1948 NAIB national championship.

Wesley Cox
Louisville (1973-77), Golden State Warriors (1977-79)
A first round pick in 1977, Cox played two seasons in the NBA with Golden State. Scored 342 points in 74 career games. Earned All-America honors in 1977 for U of L when he averaged 16.5 points for the Cardinals.

Jerry Eaves
Louisville (1978-82), Utah Jazz (1982-87), Sacramento Kings (1986-87)
A third round draft pick, Eaves played three seasons in the NBA with two teams. Averaged 9.3 ppg as a rookie with the Utah Jazz. Starting guard for Cards' 1980 NCAA Championship team. Currently an assistant coach with the New Jersey Nets.

Pervis Ellison
Louisville (1985-89), Sacramento Kings (1989-90), Washington Bullets (1990-94), Boston Celtics (1994-96)
Top pick of the 1989 draft to Sacramento, where he played one season. Named the NBA's Most Improved Player in 1991-92 with the Bullets when he averaged 20 points, 11.2 rebounds and 2.7 blocks. Totalled 377 points and 309 boards in 55 games last year with Boston.

Lancaster Gordon
Louisville (1980-84), Los Angeles Clippers (1984-88)
The eighth player taken overall in the 1984 NBA draft, he played four seasons with the Los Angeles Clippers. Single-game scoring high was 33 points on March 17, 1987 against Portland. Totalled 1,125 points in 201 games for his career.

Darrell Griffith
Louisville (1976-80), Utah Jazz (1980-91)
Second overall pick of the 1980 draft to the Utah Jazz, where he played his entire 10-year career. Named 1981 NBA Rookie of the Year when he averaged 20.6 ppg. Finished his NBA career with 12,391 points in 765 games. Career scoring leader at U of L (2,333 points).

Mike Grosso
Louisville (1968-70), Pittsburgh (1971-72)
Played one season with Pittsburgh of the ABA, scoring 104 points in 25 games. Led the Cardinals twice in rebounding with each year ranking among U of L's top ten single season efforts (432 in '68-69; 376 in '69-70).

Charles Jones
Louisville (1980-84), Phoenix Suns (1984-86), Portland Trailblazers (1986-87), Washington Bullets (1988-89)
Second in career blocked shots at U of L (208), Jones played four seasons in the NBA. Averaged 8.4 ppg and 5.1 rpg his rookie year with Phoenix. Totalled 1,015 points in 201 career NBA games over four years.

Rodney McCray
Louisville (1979-83), Houston Rockets (1983-88), Sacramento Kings (1988-90), Dallas Mavericks (1990-92), Chicago Bulls (1992-93)
Played 10 seasons in the NBA, his last as a member of the World Champion Chicago Bulls in 1992-93. Honored on the NBA's All-Defensive team in 1988. Led the NBA in minutes played in 1989-90 with the Sacramento Kings.

Scooter McCray
Louisville (1978-83), Seattle SuperSonics (1983-84), Cleveland Cavaliers (1986-87)
A second round draft pick, McCray played two seasons in the NBA. He had his best pro season in his rookie year with Seattle, when he scored 129 points in 47 games. Ranks 11th among U of L's all-time career assist leaders (349). Currently an assistant coach with the Cardinals.

Greg Minor
Louisville (1991-94), Boston Celtics (1994-96)
Member of the Celtics the last two seasons after being drafted 25th overall by the L.A. Clippers and then traded to the Indiana Pacers. Scored 31 points in his first starting assignment with the Celtics (1-28-95). Averaged 9.6 points in 78 games for the Celtics last year. Scored 1,199 points in his career with the Cards.

Dwayne Morton
Louisville (1991-94), Golden St. Warriors (1994-95)
Earned a spot on the Golden State roster after being chosen in the second round in 1994 (45th pick overall). Played in 41 games in '94-95, starting six, while totalling 167 points and 58 rebounds. U of L's all-time leader in three-point field goal percentage (.461), scoring 1,428 career points.

Allen Murphy
Louisville (1972-75), Kentucky Colonels (1975-76)
Played one season with the Kentucky Colonels before a knee injury cut his career short. He scored 113 points in 29 games for Kentucky in the 1975-76 ABA season. Led the Cardinals to the 1975 Final Four.

Chuck Noble
Louisville (1951-54), Ft. Wayne (1955-57), Detroit (1957-62)
Played seven seasons in the NBA with two teams. He began his pro career with Fort Wayne, averaging 9.5 points as a rookie. He had his best season as a pro with Detroit when he averaged 11.3 ppg. Totalled 3,276 points in 411 games for his career.

Bud Olsen
Louisville (1959-62), Cincinnati (1962-66), San Francisco (1965-67), Seattle (1967-68), Boston (1968-69), Detroit (1968-69), Kentucky Colonels (1969-70)
A seven-year player in the NBA for six different teams. Olsen enjoyed his best season as a pro when he averaged 7.5 ppg for Cincinnati in 1964-65. Totalled 1,935 points in 453 games during his pro career.

Kenny Payne
Louisville (1985-89), Philadelphia 76ers (1989-93)
A first round pick in 1989 (19th overall pick), Payne played three and a half seasons with the Philadelphia 76ers. Totalled 424 points in 131 games in his career. Second in U of L career three point field goal percentage (.401).

Jim Price
Louisville (1969-72), Los Angeles Lakers (1972-75), Milwaukee Bucks (1974-77), Denver Nuggets (1976-78), Detroit Pistons (1977-78), Los Angeles (1978-79)
Earned NBA All-Rookie team honors in 1973 with the Los Angeles Lakers. Named to the NBA All-Defensive team the following year, averaging 15.2 ppg. Price made the 1975 NBA All-Star Team as a member of the Milwaukee Bucks.

Phil Rollins
Louisville (1952-56), Philadelphia (1958-59), Cincinnati Royals (1958-61), St. Louis (1960-61), New York (1960-61)
Played three years in the NBA with four different teams. In the 1959-60 season, he enjoyed his best season as a pro in scoring 393 points in 72 games (5.5 ppg average). Starting guard on U of L's 1956 NIT Championship team.

Clifford Rozier
Louisville (1992-94), Golden St. Warriors (1994-96)
First-round draft choice of the Warriors in 1994 (16th pick overall). Started 34 games as a rookie, averaging 6.8 points and 7.4 rebounds; averaged 3.1 pts. in 59 games last year. Consensus first team All-America in 1994, producing 41 scoring and rebounding double-doubles in two seasons at U of L.

Derek Smith
Louisville (1978-82); San Diego/L.A. Clippers (1982-86); Sacramento (1986-89), Philadelphia 76ers (1989-90), Boston Celtics (1990-91)
Smith's best season was 1984-85 with the L.A. Clippers when he averaged 22.1 ppg and ranked among the top five NBA guards in rebounds, FG percentage, scoring and blocked shots. Totalled 4,563 points in 333 games over nine seasons.

LaBradford Smith
Louisville (1987-91), Washington Bullets (1991-93), Sacramento Kings (1993-94)
A 1991 first-round NBA draft pick (19th overall), Smith averaged 9.3 ppg in 1993-94, his second with the Bullets. He scored a career-high 37 points at Chicago (March 19, 1993). U of L's all-time assist leader (713) and career free throw percentage leader (.866).

Felton Spencer
Louisville (1986-90), Minn. Timberwolves (1990-93), Utah Jazz (1993-96), Orlando Magic (1996-)
Played three years with the Minnesota Timberwolves. Traded to the Utah Jazz in 1993 where he started at center the last three years. Traded to Orlando in the off-season. Totalled 9,258 career points in 6 seasons. Holds the U of L record for career FG pct. (.628).

Ron Thomas
Louisville (1970-1972), Kentucky Colonels (1972-76)
Thomas played for the Kentucky Colonels of the ABA for four years. He totalled 1,051 points in 264 games during his his four-year career with the Colonels. Thomas was the last U of L player to average double figures in rebounding (13.5) for the Cards until Clifford Rozier averaged 10.9 in '92-93.

Billy Thompson
Louisville (1982-1986), Los Angeles Lakers (1986-88), Miami Heat (1988-91)
A member of the NBA Champion L.A. Lakers in 1987, where he became one of only four players to have played on an NCAA Championship and NBA Championship team in back-to-back years. Totalled 2,580 career points in 322 games.

John Turner
Louisville (1958-61), Chicago Bulls (1961-62)
An All-America pick for the Cardinals in 1961, Turner played one season in the NBA with Chicago, scoring 200 points in 42 games during the 1961-62 season. His 669 points scored as a senior (23.1 avg.) is the third highest ever in a season at U of L.

Charlie Tyra
Louisville (1953-57), New York (1957-61), Chicago (1961-62)
A two-time consensus All-America pick at U of L, Tyra played five years in NBA, four with New York and one in Chicago. Originally drafted by Detroit, Tyra averaged a season-best 12.8 ppg in 74 games with New York in 1959-60. Tyra scored 3,091 points in his 348 pro career games.

Wes Unseld
Louisville (1965-68); Washington Bullets (1968-81)
Played 13 years for the Baltimore/Washington Bullets. Second player in NBA history to be chosen NBA Rookie of the Year and Most Valuable Player in the same season. Named Championship Series MVP in leading the Bullets to the 1978 NBA title. Enshrined in the Pro Basketball Hall of Fame in 1988.

Milt Wagner
Louisville (1981-86), Los Angeles Lakers (1977-78)
Third on Cardinals' all-time scoring list (1,834 points), Wagner played one year in the NBA with the 1988 World Champion Los Angeles Lakers, averaging 3.8 ppg as a reserve guard. He has also played several seasons in the CBA and is currently playing professional basketball in Israel.

Samaki Walker
Louisville (1994-96), Dallas Mavericks (1996)
Drafted with the ninth pick overall by the Mavericks following his sophomore season at U of L. Recorded the only triple-double in U of L history with a 14-point, 10-rebound, 11-blocked shots performance against Kentucky as a freshman (1-1-95).

Rick Wilson
Louisville (1974-78), Atlanta Hawks (1978-80)
Wilson played two years with the Atlanta Hawks. A 1978 second round draft pick, he played every position but center in his two-year NBA career. Twice in the 1978-79 season, he scored personal NBA career highs of ten points against Golden State and Portland.

WHERE THEY ARE NOW

The following is a partial list of U of L players who lettered in basketball. Where information is available, their occupations and residence is listed. If you have additional information on other U of L lettermen, or updated information on the players listed, please contact the Louisville Sports Information office by calling (502) 852-6581.

Able, Forrest — (1952) Fairdale High School, Louisville, KY

Abram, Mike — (1988) Private Business, Louisville, KY

Akridge, Bill — (1964, BA) Chaplain, US Army, Ft. Bennings, GA

Alexander, Rick — (1974, BSC) Vice President, CEO, Armor Elevator, Louisville, KY

Andrews, Aaron — (1942) Retired College Administrator, Big Rapids, MI

Andrews, Harley — (1960) Self-employed, Clay City, TN

Andrews, Harold — (1959) Retired, Principal, Louisville, KY

Arnold, Andrew — (1972) Dentist, Princeton, KY

Avery, Charles — (1940) Retired, Petroleum Landman, Plano, TX

Bacon, Henry — (1972) AAA Regional Sales Manager, Bowling Green, KY

Basham, Paul — (1956) Sales Mgr. - Boone Steel Corp., Ft. Thomas, KY

Bass, Lewis (Sonny) — (1944) Retired Realtor, Louisville, KY

Beam, Chet — (1958) Sales, Continental Kitchens, Kettering, OH

Beard, Butch — (1969) Head Basketball Coach, New Jersey Nets, East Rutherford, NJ

Beasley, Tom — (1939, BA) Retired, Sheridan, IN

Bergdoll, Jerry — (1965) Cardinal Filters, Louisville, KY

Bertelson, Dick — (1936) Louisville, KY

Bissmeyer, Ollie — (1949, AB) Asst. Professor, University of Kentucky, Lexington, KY

Blackerby, James — (1927) Retired Physician, New Bern, NC

Bohn, Robert — Dentist, Louisville, KY

Bomar, Harold — (1949, BS) Nursing Home Owner, Louisville, KY

Bond, Phillip — (1978, BSC) Vice President of Finance and Administration - Metro United Way, Louisville, KY

Borah, Bob (1949) B & B Freight, Louisville, KY

Bott, Kenny — (1932) Retired, Louisville, KY

Bradley, Ken — (1973) Retired U.S. Air Force, Las Vegas, NV

Branch, Tony — (1980) Iroquois High School, Louisville, KY

James Brewer — Professional basketball in Hungary

Bridgeman, Junior — (1975, BA) Wendy's Franchisee, Louisville, KY

Britt, Frank — (1941) Superintendent - Electric Distribution Dept., LG&E, Louisville, KY

Brohm, Charles — (1960) Physician, Prospect, KY

Brown, Danny — (1977) Teacher, Real Estate, Excel Telecommunications, North Vernon, IN

Brown, Wiley — (1982) Strength and Conditioning Coordinator, U of L, Louisville, KY

Bryant, Ellis — (1968, BSC) Partner, Anderson, Bryant, Lasky & Winslow, CPA, Louisville, KY

Bryant, Thomas — (1952) Sales Rep., Lexington, KY

Bugg, Steve — (1980) Special Agent, U.S. Secret Service, Louisville, KY

Bunton, Bill — (1975) Chamber of Commerce, Louisville, KY

Bunton, Stanley — (1977) Restaurant Manager, Louisville, KY

Burman, Carl — (1949) Retired, Civil Service, Trotwood, OH

Burkman, Roger — (1981) Director of Development, Trinity High School, Louisville, KY

Burnette, George — (1958) Insurance Agent, Mayfield, KY

Butler, Bill — (1974) High School Coach and Teacher, Miami, FL

Butler, Don — (1921, DDS) Dentist, Sullivan, IN

Butters, Ken — (1967) Orthopedic Surgeon, Eugene, OR

Calhoun, Doug — (1994) Commercial Account Executive for GTE, Henderson, KY

Callahan, Paul — (1969) Athletic Director, Seneca High School, Louisville, KY

Carleton, John — (1945) Physician, Santa Barbara, CA

Carroll, Michael — (1975) Self Employed, Louisville, KY

Carter, Larry — (1972) Owner, Carter and Lawrence, Louisville, KY

Case, Mike — (1993) Assistant Manager, Enterprise Rent-A-Car, Anderson, IN

Clark, Norman — (1947, BS) President, Derby City Auto Supply, Louisville, KY

Clark, Steve — (1981) Supermarket Subcontractor, Matthews, NC

Cleveland, Daryl — (1980) Hamilton Printing, Louisville, KY

Clifford, Dennis — (1965) Troy, Mich.

Clore, C.A. — (1934, BSCE) Retired, Louisville, KY

Coleman, Jack — (1950, BS) Building Materials Dealer, Burgin, KY

Compton, Deward — (1948, BA) Retired, Account Executive, Murfreesboro, TN

Corrin, Ralph — (1945, BCE) V.P. Bristol Steel & Iron Works, Bristol, TN

Corso, Marty — (1926, DDS) Dentist, Mayfield Heights, OH

Cosby, Wayne — (1977) Construction, Louisville, KY

Cox, Corky — (1954, BS) Retired High School Principal, Hodgensville, KY

Cox, Wesley — (1977) Teacher, Louisville, KY

Crawley, John — (1971) Louisville, KY

Creamer, Eddie — (1954) U.S. Secret Service, Nashville, TN

Crook, Herbert — (1988) Professional basketball in Finland

Cummings, James — (1939) Retired, Graham, TX

Daniel, Maurice — (1918, BS) Retired, U.S. Army, Sarasota FL

Darragh, Bill — (1957, BS) Owner, Long John Silvers and Rally's Franchises, Louisville, KY

Daubert, H.T. — (1932, AB) Retired, Louisville, KY

Deeken, Dennis — (1969) Owner of Insectaway Systems of Kentucky Inc., Louisville, KY

Demoisey, Truett R. — (1933) Walton, KY

Deuser, Greg — (1982) Manager, Investment Firm, Louisville, KY

Dick, Kenny — (1934) Insurance Salesman, Anchorage, KY

Doctor, Richard — (1961) Hospital Engineer, Philadelphia, PA

Doll, Kenny — (1936) Retired, Louisville, KY

Donohue, Steve — (1980) Athletic Trainer, New York Yankees, Bronx, NY

Dotson, William — (1938) Retired, Louisville, KY

Doutaz, Denny — (1967) High School Basketball Coach/Teacher, Forest Park, IN

Dunbar, Bob — (1953) Retired, Indianapolis, IN

Eaves, Jerry — (1982) Asst. Basketball Coach, University of Louisville, Louisville, KY

Edwards, Jim — (1951) Retired, Paducah, KY

Eichenholz, Leon — (1934) Retired Judge, Louisville, KY

Ehringer, Dave — (1960, BA) Board of Directors, Citizens Bank, IN

Ellerkamp, George — (1942) Retired Foreman at Brown-Foreman Distillery, Louisville, KY

Ellis, Jim — (1978) Attorney, Louisville, KY

Ellis, John — (1973) Orthopedic surgeon, Louisville, KY

Ellison, Pervis — (1989) Pro Basketball, Boston Celtics, Boston, MA

Epley, Frank — (1948, BA) Optician, Lexington, KY

Eschrich, John — (1914, BA) Retired, Louisville, KY

Finn, John — (1957) President, Howden Sirocco, Dundee, OH

Finnegan, Tom — (1965, BS) Teacher, Moore High School, Louisville, KY

Ford, Leon — (1952) Retired, Montgomery, AL

Forrest, Manuel — (1985) Professional Basketball in South America

Fraley, Shannon — (1990) Self-employed, Somerset, KY

Francis, Hugh — (1943, BA) Retired, Louisville, KY

Frazier, Jadie — (1963, BS) Retired, Owns & manages softball park & farm, Louisville, KY

Frazer, Joey — (1983, BA) Washington, DC

Froning, John L. (1958) Dentist, Crestwood, KY

Gallon, Ricky — City of Tampa Recreation Department, Tampa, FL

Gastevich, Vladimir — (1955) Attorney, Crown Point, IN

Giannini, Tom — (1934) Physician, Louisville, KY

Girdler, Reynolds — (1926) Riverside, CT

Givens, Ambrose — (1947) President, Clay Ingels, Co., Lexington, KY

Glaza, Al — (1957, BA) Petroleum Dealer, Springfield, IL

Goldstein, Don — (1959, BA) Dentist, Melville, NY

Goodman, Joseph — (1949) Retired, Louisville, KY

Gordon, Lancaster — (1983) Salvation Army Boys and Girls Club, Louisville, KY

Grandmission, Albert — (1938, DMD) Dentist, North Andover, MA

Griffith, Darrell — (1980) Self-Employed, Louisville, KY

Grosso, Mike — (1970) Account Executive, WHAS-TV, Louisville, KY

Grubbs, Frank — (1933, AB) Retired Attorney, Louisville, KY

Hagan, Charles — (1971) Attorney/Interior Designer, Louisville, KY

Hale, Fred — (1975) International Harvester, Sales, Louisville, KY

Hall, Dave — (1964) Owner, Cardinal Medical Corp., Louisville, KY

Hall, Jeff — (1986) Self-employed, Louisville, KY

Harmon, Bill — (1977) Owner, President, Harmon Construction Co., North Vernon, IN

Harrah, Herb — (1956, BS) Retired, Dewey, IL

Harris, William — (1941) Retired, High Point, NC

Hauptfuhrer, George — (1946) Attorney, Philadelphia, PA

Hawley, Craig — (1990) Attorney, Louisville, KY

Hawley, Ron — (1964, BS) Special Agent, FBI, Westfield, IN

Cornelius Holden — (1992) Professional Basketball in Europe

Holden, Fred — (1968, MA) Teacher, Manual High School, Louisville, KY

Holland, Gary — (1969, BS) Teacher, Basketball Coach, Spring Valley H.S., French Lick, IN

Horine, Elwyn — (1940, AB) President, D.A. Hines Co., Lynchburg, VA

Houston, Wade — (1966, BS) Owner Trucking Company, Louisville, KY

Howard, Terry — (1975) Insurance Sales, Louisville, KY

Hutt, Joe — (1945) Retired, Louisville, KY

Jensen, Louis — (1950) Counselor, Coach, New Albany, IN

Jeter, James — (1985) United Parcel Service, Louisville, KY

Johnson, George — (1938, AB) Retired General Surgeon, Richmond, IN

Johnson, Oz — (1948) Jefferson County Board of Education, Louisville, KY

Jones, Charles — (1984) Police Office, City of Louisville, Elizabethtown, KY

Jones, Kent — (1985) Police Officer, City of Louisville, Louisville, KY

Kalkhof, Skip — (1979) Business Manager, Bausch & Lomb, Indian Springs, OH

Kasdan, Martin — (1941) Louisville, KY

Keeling, Crawford — (1938, BA) Retired, V.P. Treasurer, Avery Federal Savings & Loan, Louisville, KY

Keller, William — (1927) Retired Physician, Louisville, KY

Kelsey, Jerry — (1959) Sales, KY

Kidd, Bill — (1953, MEd) Teacher, Southern High School, Louisville, KY

Kimbro, Tony — (1990) City of Louisville Recreation Department

King, Jerry — (1969) Vice President, Sales, Kentucky Lottery, Louisville, KY

King, Robert — (1941) Retired, Louisville, KY

Kinker, Don — (1946, BSME) Retired Auto Executive, Howell, MI

Kinnaird, Tony — (1977) Hamilton Printing Co., Louisville, KY

Kirchdorfer, Norb — (1934) Retired, V.P. Reynolds Metal Co., Louisville, KY

Kraft, Ted — (1931, BSEE) Retired, Louisville, KY

Lawhon, Mike — (1972, BA) Orthopedic Surgeon, Cincinnati, OH

Leathers, Buddy — (1961) Self Employed, Louisville, KY

Lentz, Frank — (1953) Teacher, Tampa, FL

Lester, David — (1984) Sales, Louisville, KY

Liedtke, Joe — (1967) High School Liaison, Jefferson County Board of Education, Louisville, KY

Linonis, Ed — (1969, BSC) Sales, Hardware Supplies, All State Dist., Youngstown, OH

Lochmueller, Bob — (1952, BS) Head Health, Phys. Ed., Drivers Ed. Dept., Tell City, IN

Lockwood, John (1972) Airline Pilot, Northwest Airlines, Poway, CA

Loehle, Larry — (1977, MD) Physician, Louisville, KY

Long, Harry — (1936) Retired, Auto Dealer, Shelbyville, KY

Mahaffey, D. E. — (1946, MD) Physician, Louisville, KY

Maish, Orville Sr. — (1945, BD) Minister, First Church of the Nazarene, Mason, MI

Tim Marcum - (1975) Construction Project Manager, Louisville, KY

Mantel, Alex — (1960, BA) Dentist, Easton, CT

Mattingly, Buddy — (1971) Controller, Tumbleweed Restaurant, Louisville, KY

May, Jerry — (1974) Athletic Trainer, University of Louisville

McCray, Rodney — (1983) Houston, TX

McCray, Scooter — (1983) Asst. Basketball Coach, University of Louisville

McLendon, Jason — (1992) Private Business, Ft. Myers, FL

McSwain, Johnny — (1976) Firefighter, Atlanta, GA

McSwain, Mark — (1987) Professional Basketball in France

Meiman, Joe — (1973, BSC) Sales Manager, Monroe Systems Co., Louisville, KY

Meiman, John — (1978) Account Executive, Bell South Business Systems, Louisville, KY

Metcalf, Harold — (1951) Retired, Phoeniz, AZ

Miles, Rick — (1973) Physician, Russell Springs, KY

Minner, Gordon — (1968) Retired USAF Pilot, Dover, DE

Minor, Greg — (1994) Professional Basketball, Boston Celtics, Boston, MA

Mitchell, Danny — (1985) Teacher, North Harrison High School, English, IN

Monen, Si — (1938) Owner, Sterling Shop, Chattanooga, TN

Morgan, Jim — (1957, BS) Trainer, Thoroughbreds, Owner, Wendevoer Farm, Bellbrook, OH

Moriarty, John — (1928) Louisville, KY

Morton, Dwayne — (1994) Professional Basketball in Israel

Mouser, Steve — (1975) Teacher, Louisville, KY

Muldoon, Phil — (1947, LLB) Deputy Dir. of Collections, Cincinnati, OH

Murphy, Allen — (1977) Youth Director, Birmingham, AL

Musterman, Ed — (1936) Retired Engineer, Louisville, KY

Naber, Bob — (1952) Covington, KY

Nalevanko, Charles — (1970) Teacher, Head Basketball Coach, Louisville, KY

Neely, Greg — (1971, BA) Attorney, New Albany, IN

Newkirk, Richard — (1919) Louisville, KY

Noble, Chuck — (1954) Owner, Cenco Services, Fresno, CA

Nuss, David — (1965) Supervisor, Sun Micro Systems, Inc., Lexington, MA

Olliges, Will — (1988) Financial Planner, Louisville, KY

Olsen, Bud — (1962) Louisville, KY

Ogden, James — (1936), DMD, Retired, Cincinnati, OH

Osborn, John — (1949, LLB) Attorney, Louisville, KY

Otte, H. F. — (1947) Covington, KY

Panther, Bud — (1938) Retired, Louisville, KY

Panther, Dick — (1939) Retired, Louisville, KY

Parker, Clyde — (1946, DMD) Retired Dentist, Evansville, IN

Payne, Kenny — (1989) Professional Basketball in Japan

Peloff, Dick — (1963, BS) Owner, Printsley Creations Screen Printing Co., Carmel, IN

Peyton, Thomas — (1942) Retired, Hospital Administrator, Chapel Hill, NC

Phelps, Tanny — (1961) Optician, Richmond, KY

Phillips, William — (1942) Retired, Louisville, KY

Pickett, Jeffrey — (1982) Teacher, Coach, Shepherdsville, KY

Pike, Hal — (1955) Minister, Covington, KY

Potts, C. Ray — (1949) Semi-Retired, Physician, Louisville, KY

Powell, Bill — (1955, BS) Self-employed, Louisville, KY

Powell, Nelson — (1963) US Air Force Reserved, Marietta, GA

Price, Greg — (1973) Attorney, Louisville, KY

Price, Jim — (1972) Asst. Coach, Butler University, Indianapolis, IN

Protenic, Jim — (1975) Athletic Director, Teacher, Presentation Academy, Louisville, KY

Prudhoe, John — (1955, BS) Accountant, Caterpillar Tractor Co., East Peoria, IL

Pry, Paul — (1972, BSC) Terminal Manager, Smith's Transfer Corp., Newburg, NY

Pulliam, Marty — (1982) Pressman, Danville, KY

Quisenberry, Ken — (1991) Building Manager, U of L, Louisville, KY

Ray, Jack — (1962) Candy Manufacturer, Altoona, PA

Raymond, R. H. — (1943, BS) President, Richard Raymonds, Assoc., Melno Park, CA

Reschar, John — (1954) Retired, Louisville, KY

Reeves, Kenny — (1950, BA) Dentist, Louisville, KY

Reid, Ben — (1933, MD) Retired, Physician, Louisville, KY

Reuther, John — (1965) Teacher, Louisville, KY

Reuther, Joseph — (1964) Systems Operator, Ford Motor Co., Louisville, KY

Ries, Bob — (1948, BME) Regional Manager, Allegheny Ludlum, Arlington Heights, IL

Robinson, David — (1989) Pro Basketball in Columbia

Robison, Dick — (1958) Brownstown, IN

Rollins, Phil — (1956, BS) Cissna Sporting Goods, Louisville, KY

Rooks, Ron — (1965, BS) Teacher, Loveland, OH

Roth, Horace — (1930) Semi-Retired Attorney, Prospect, KY

Rothman, Judd — (1965) Partner, Principal; Rothman and Rothman, CPA's, Patchogue, NY

Scott, Edwin (1933) Physician, Attorney, Louisville, KY

Search, Ted — (1952, BS) President, Chester Chrysler-Plymouth Co., Chester, IL

Selvy, Marv — (1969) Petroleum Equipment Sales, Louisville, KY

Shackelford, Roscoe — (1957) Retired, Superintendent, Hazard, KY

Sipe, Kenny — (1942, BCHE) Sales Rep., Reliance Universal, Morristown, NJ

Smith, Dave — (1978) CPA, Louisville, KY

Smith, LaBradford — (1991) Pro basketball, CBA Quad City Thunder

Smith, Troy — (1993) Professional Basketball in France

Snively, Curtis — (1991) Sales, Louisville, KY

Snyder, Alva — (1929, DDS) Ashland, KY

Sosnin, Hershell — (1934) Jenkintown, PA

South, Reagan — (1941, MD) Physician, San Francisco, CA

Spencer, Charlie — (1930) Retired, Louisville, KY

Spencer, Felton — (1990) Pro Basketball, Orlando Magic, Orlando, FL

Stacey, Howard — (1962) Manager Iowa Realty, INC., Des Moines, IA

Stallings, Ron — (1972) U.S. Marine Corps

Steltenkamp, Thomas — (1985) Certified Athletic Trainer, Rudy Ellis Sports Medicine Clinic, Louisville, KY

Stripling, Jon — (1963) Retired, NASA, Pocomoke City, MD

Stultz, Elwood — (1970, DMD) Retired, Owensboro, KY

Stultz, John — (1940, BA) Louisville, KY

Sullivan, Everick — (1992) Professional Basketball in Greece

Summers, Harold — (1942) Airline Pilot, Delta Airlines, East Point, GA

Terrell, Bob — (1953) President, Fred Jones Electronics, Oklahoma City, OK

Thomas, Ron — (1972) Louisville, KY

Thompson, Billy — (1986) Pro Basketball in Israel

Threlkeld, Bill — (1935, AB) Retired, Dallas, TX

Tieman, Roger — (1960, BS) Retired, Deputy Property Evaluator, Covington, KY

Trenholme, William — (1946, BEE) Senior Engineer, Mountain States Mineral Enterprise, Tuscon, AZ

Turner, John — (1961) Retired, Newport, KY

Tyra, Charlie — (1957, BS) Sales, St. Joe Paper Co., Louisville, KY

Unseld, Wes — (1968) Community Relations Director, Washington Bullets, Washington, DC

Valentine, Robbie — (1986) Sports Director, Boy Scouts of America, Louisville, KY

Vance, Bruce — (1923, BS) Retired Supervisor, Louisville Public Schools, Louisville, KY

Vari, Frank — (1966) Golf Sales, Dayton, OH

Varoscak, John — (1958) Dean of Students, Pittsburgh Public Schools, Pittsburgh, PA

Vilcheck, Al — (1972) casino employee, Reno, NV

Waggener, Gil — (1950) Owner, Waggener Farms, Burgin, KY

Wagner, Alfred — (1940) Retired Physician, Anchorage, KY

Wagner, Milt — (1986) Pro Basketball in Israel

Watkins, Jerry — (1961) Retired, Risk Manager, Louisville Water Co, Louisville, KY

Webb, Derwin — (1993) U of L Law School, Louisville, KY

Weber, Robert — (1940) Retired, Purchasing Mgmt., Louisville, KY

Wedekind, J.B. — (1937) Retired, Bay Village, OH

Wellman, Bob — (1952, BS) V.P. Southern Optical Co., Louisville, KY

West, Chris — (1986) Boy Scouts, Louisville, KY

White, David — (1950) Church Administrator (Asst. Gen. Secretary), Nashville, TN

Whitfield, Ike — (1975) Recreation Director, Long Beach, CA

Whitehead, Eddie — (1966) Broadcasting, General Manager, Miramar, FL

Wilkie, Ray — (1947, BA) Psychologist, Instructor, University of Kentucky, Lexington, KY

Williams, Harlan — (1951, BS) Teacher, Douglas County Schools, Castle Rock, CO

Williams, Keith — (1990) Sales, Xerox Corp., Louisville, KY

Williams, Larry — (1979) Youth Development Coordinator, Housing Authority of Louisville

Willig, Armin — (1934, BA) Retired, Louisville, KY

Willingter, Paul — (1939, BA) Guidance Counselor, Manual High School, Louisville, KY

Wright, Les — (1934, AB) Retired President, Samford University, Birmingham, AL

Wright, Poncho — (1982) Contractor, Indianapolis, IN

York, Cliff — (1954) Sales, 3-M Company, Louisville, KY

Zeller, Rod — (1944, BCE) President, Wehr Construction Inc., Louisville, KY

Zirkle, Charles — (1940, JD) Attorney, Louisville, KY

LETTERMEN

A Able, Forrest 1951-52; Abram, Mike 1984-85,1985-86, 1986-87, 1987-88; Akridge, Bill 1962-63; Alberston, Bob 1977-78,1978-79; Alexander, Rick 1971-72; Andrews, Aaron 1938-39,1939-40,1940-41,1941-42; Andrews, Harold 1956-57, 1957-58, 1958-59; Armstrong, Jerry 1959-60, 1960-61, 1961-62; Atkinson, John 1918-19.

B Bacon,Henry 1969-70, 1970-71, 1971-72; Bacon, Jim 1938-39, 1939-40; Baden, Harry 1921-22, 1923-24; Baily, C. 1925-26; Bass, Lewis "Sonny" 1940-41, 1941-42; Baxter, Sam 1913-14, 1914-15; Beam, Chet 1951-52, 1952-53, 1953-54; Beard, Butch 1966-67,1967-68, 1968-69; Beasley, Tom 1935-36, 1937-38; Bein, Thomas 1935-36, 1936-37; Bern, M. 1936-37, 1937-38; Bertelson, Dick 1931-32, 1932-33, 1933-34; Bissmeyer, Ollie 1945-46; Blackerby, Jim 1923-24, 1924-25, 1925-26, 1926-27; Bomar, Harold 1944-45; Bond, Phillip 1972-73, 1974-75, 1975-76, 1976-77; Boone, C.T. 1929-30, 1930-31, 1931-32, 1932-33; Borah, Bob 1947-48, 1948-49; Bott, Kenny 1927-28, 1928-29, 1929-30, 1930-31, 1931-32; Bowen, J.W. 1945-46; Bradley, Ken 1971-72, 1972-73; Branch, Tony 1976-77, 1977-78, 1978-79, 1979-80; Brand, Fred 1935-36; Brewer, James 1988-89, 1990-91, 1991-92, 1992-93; Bridgeman, Ulysses "Junior" 1972-73, 1973-74, 1974-75; Britt, F.R. 1939-40, 1940-41; Brown, Bob 1948-49, 1949-50, 1950-51, 1951-52; Brown, Danny 1973-74, 1974-75, 1975-76, 1976-77; Brown, Wiley 1978-79, 1979-80, 1980-81, 1981-82; Browne, Kenny 1926-27, 1927-28, 1928-29; Bryant, Ellis 1965-66; Bufford, Randy 1977-78, 1978-79, 1979-80, 1980-81; Bugg, Steve 1977-78, 1978-79; Bunton, Bill 1971-72, 1972-73, 1974-75; Bunton, Stanley 1973-74, 1974-75, 1975-76, 1976-77; Burkman, Roger 1977-78, 1978-79, 1979-80, 1980-81; Butler, Bill 1972-73, 1973-74; Butler, Don 1918-19, 1919-20, 1920-21.

C Caine, John 1946-47; Caldwell, C.N. 1911-12, 1912-13, 1913-14; Caldwell, J.P. 1911-12; Calhoun, Doug 1991-92, 1992-93, 1993-94; Carleton, John 1944-45; Carter, Larry 1969-70, 1970-71, 1971-72; Carter, Horace 1919-20, 1920-21, 1921-22; Case, Mike 1989-90, 1990-91, 1991-92, 199293; Chappell, Joe 1928-29; Clark, Norman 1944-45; Clark, Rick 1982-83, 1983-84; Clark, Steve 1979-80, 1980-81; Clark, William 1945-46; Claydon, Howard 1923-24; Cleveland, Daryl 1977-78, 1978-79, 1979-80; Clifford, Dennis 1962-63, 1963-64, 1964-65; Clore, C.A. 1932-33, 1933-34; Coleman, Jack 1946-47, 1947-48, 1948-49; Combs, Glenn 1946-47, 1947-48, 1948-49, 1949-50; Combs, Roy 1946-47, 1947-48, 1948-49, 1949-50; Compton, Deward 1946-47, 1947-48; Cooper, Tim 1971-72, 1972-73; Corrin, Ralph 1944-45; Corso, Marty 1921-22, 1925-26; Cosby, Wayne 1975-76; Cox, Corky 1951-52, 1952-53, 1953-54; Cox, Wesley 1973-74, 1974-75, 1975-76, 1976-77; Craddock, Ed 1925-26, 1926-27, 1927-28, 1928-29; Craik, James 1939-40; Creamer, Eddie 1963-64, 1964-65; Crook, Herbert 1984-85, 1985-86, 1986-87, 1987-88.

D Damel, John 1911-12, 1912-13, 1913-14, 1914-15; Daniel, Maurice 1913-14, 1914-15; Daniel, Roy 1914-15, 1915-16, 1917-18; Dantzler, Damion 1994-95; Darragh, Bill 1954-55, 1955-56, 1956-57; Daubert, H.T. 1927-28, 1929-30, 1930-31, 1931-32; Davis, John 1943-44; Deaton, Charles 1956-57; Deeken, Dennis 1966-67, 1967-68, 1968-69;

Demoisey, Kenny 1930-31, 1931-32, 1932-33; Deuser, Greg 1977-78, 1979-80, 1980-81, 1981-82; Dick, Kenney 1930-31, 1931-32, 1932-33; Doll, Kenny 1933-34, 1934-35, 1935-36; Doll, Paul 1934-35, 1935-36, 1936-37; Doutaz, Bobby 1963-64; Doutaz, Denny 1965-66; Drake,B.I. 1939-40; Dunbar, Bob 1950-51; Dunbar, Frank 1947-48; Dunweg, Rudy 1912-13; DuPont, Jerry 1955-56, 1956-57, 1957-58.

E Eaves, Jerry 1978-79, 1979-80, 1980-81, 1981-82; Edwards, Jim 1947-48, 1948-49, 1949-50, 1950-51; Ehringer, Dave 1956-57; Ellis, Jim 1977-78; Ellis, John 1971-72, 1972-73; Ellison, Pervis 1985-86, 1986-87, 1987-88, 1988-89; Engelhard, Warren 1943-44; Epley, Frank 1940-41, 1941-42, 1946-47; Eschrich, John 1911-12,1912-13,1913-14; Epsie, Marshall 1926-27; Estes, Jim 1936-37.

F Farmer, Craig 1994-95; Finnegan, Tom 1963-64, 1964-65; Flynn, B.J. 1994-95; Flynn J.F. 1945-46, 1946-47, 1947-48; Ford, Leon 1948-49, 1949-50, 1950-51, 1951-52; Ford, Tom 1926-27; Forrest, Manuel 1981-82, 1983-84, 1984-85; Foster, Owen 1912-13, 1914-15; Fraley, Shannon 1987-88, 1988-89, 1989-90; Francis, Hugh 1939-40; Franks, W.T. 1938-39; Frazer, Joey 1980-81; Frazier, Jadie 1960-61, 1961-62, 1962-63; Frazier, Lanham 1938-39, 1939-40; Freeman, R.S. 1943-44.

G Gallon, Rick 1974-75, 1975-76, 1976-77, 1977-78; Gans, Harry 1938-39, 1939-40; Garwitz, Bob 1945-46; Gastevich, Vlad 1952-53, 1953-54, 1954-55; Geiling, Bill, 1958-59; Gentile, John 1924-25, 1925-26; Giannini, Tom 1930-31, 1931-32, 1933-34; Gilbert, Dave 1964-65, 1965-66, 1966-67; Gillim, D.L. 1943-44; Gilstrap, Curt 1975-76; Girdler, Reynolds 1924-25; Givens, Ambrose 1943-44; Glaza, Al 1954-55, 1955-56, 1956-57; Goldstein, Don 1956-57, 1957-58, 1958-59; Gordon, Lancaster 1980-81, 1981-82, 1982-83,1983-84; Gorius, Bob 1965-66, 1966-67, 1967-68; Grandmaison, Albert 1935-36; Griffith, Danny 1980-81; Griffith, Darrell 1976-77, 1977-78, 1978-79, 1979-80; Grimes, "Red" 1913-14; Grosso, Mike 1968-69, 1969-70; Grubbs, Frank 1932-33.

H Haas, Danny 1983-84, 1984-85, 1985-86, 1986-87; Hagan, Charles 1970-71; Hall, Bob 1928-29, 1929-30; Hall, Dave 1960-61, 1961-62, 1962-63, 1963-64; Hall, Emmett 1913-14; Hall, Jeff 1982-83, 1983-84, 1984-85, 1985-86; Hampton, Tom 1937-38; Harmon, Bill 1973-74, 1974-75, 1975-76, 1976-77; Harmon, Jerome 1989-90; Harrah, Herb 1952-53, 1953-54, 1954-55, 1955-56; Harris, Bill 1939-40, 1941-42; Hauptfuhrer, George 1944-45, 1945-46; Hawley, Craig 1986-87, 1987-88, 1988-89, 1989-90; Hawley, Ron 1961-62, 1962-63, 1963-64; Haws, Watson 1923-24; Hecht, Bobby 1982-83, 1983-84, 1984-85; Heft, Ivan 1911-12; Helm, George 1936-37; Herzer, G.C. 1917-18, 1918-19, 1919-20, 1920-21; Hill, George 1919-20, 1920-21; Hinton, Harry 1952-53, 1953-54; Hocker, Al 1923-24; Hocker, Charles 1919-20, 1920-21, 1921-22; Hoffman, George 1938-39; Holden, Cornelius 1988-89, 1989-90, 1990-91, 1991-92; Holden, Fred 1965-66, 1966-67, 1967-68; Holland, Gary 1967-68, 1968-69; Hopgood, Brian 1991-92, 1992-93; Horine, Elwyn 1937-38, 1938-39, 1939-40; Houle, Rollin 1943-44; Houston, Wade 1963-64, 1964-65, 1965-66; Howard, Terry 1972-73, 1973-74, 1974-75; Howard, Todd 1989-90, 1990-91; Hunter, Dick 1945-46;

Hutt, Joe 1940-41, 1944-45.

I Imorde, Bill 1930-31, 1934-35; Ingram, Delno 1937-38, 1938-39.

J Jefferson, Carlyle 1911-12; Jensen, Louis 1949-50; Jeter, James 1981-82, 1982-83, 1983-84, 1984-85; Johnson, Cal 1944-45, 1945-46; Johnson, Eric 1994-95; Johnson, George 1935-36; Johnson, Jack 1943-44; Johnson, Oz 1946-47, 1947-48; Jones, Charles 1980-81, 1981-82, 1982-83, 1983-84; Jones, Frank 1919-20, 1920-21, 1921-22; Jones, Kent 1981-82, 1982-83, 1983-84, 1984-85; Judy, Raymond 1931-32.

K Kasden, Marty 1939-40; Keeling, Crawford 1935-36; Keffer, Bill 1952-53, 1953-54, 1954-55, 1955-56; Kelly, Mickey 1957-58; Kemp, C.W. 1928-29, 1929-30; Kennedy, J.L. 1928-29; Kessler, Frank 1920-21; Kidd, Bill 1948-49; Kienzle, Tommy 1919-20,1920-21, 1921-22; Kimbro, Tony 1985-86, 1986-87, 1988-89, 1989-90; King, Jerry 1966-67, 1967-68, 1968-69; King, Jimmy 1992-93, 1993-94, 1994-95; King, Robert 1938-39, 1939-40, 1940-41; Kinker,Don 1943-44, 1944-45, 1945-46; Kinnaird, Tony 1973-74, 1974-75, 1976-77; Kirchdorfer, Norb 1932-33, 1933-34; Kirk, E.B. 1919-20; Kiser, Brian 1992-93, 1993-94, 1994-95; Kitchen, Joe 1957-58, 1958-59, 1959-60; Knopf, Johnny 1945-46, 1946-47, 1947-48, 1948-49; Kornfeld, Edwin 1913-14, 1914-15, 1915-16; Koster, Fred 1924-25, 1925-26, 1926-27, 1927-28; Kraft, Ted 1929-30; Kupper, Ed 1944-45, 1945-46, 1946-47.

L LaDurand, Jules 1917-18, 1918-19, 1919-20; Larrabee, Wayne 1950-51; Lawhon, Mike 1969-70, 1970-71, 1971-72; Leathers, Buddy 1958-59, 1959-60, 1960-61; LeGree, Keith 1991-92, 1992-93; Lester, David 1981-82, 1982-83, 1983-84; Libbey, Burt 1926-27, 1927-28, 1928-29, 1929-30; Liedtke, Joe 1964-65, 1965-66, 1966-67; Linonis, Ed 1967-68, 1968-69; Lochmueller, Bob 1949-50, 1950-51, 1951-52; Loehle, Larry 1972-73; Long, Harry 1933-34, 1934-35, 1935-36.

M Mahaffey, D.E. 1941-42; Mahaffey, J.H. 1941-42; Maish, Orville 1939-40, 1940-41; Manion, Bob 1947-48, 1948-49; Mantel, Alex 1956-57, 1957-58, 1958-59; Marks, Poachy 1924-25, 1925-26; Marshall, Avery 1986-87; Martin, Jeff 1984-85, 1985-86; Masterson, Ches 1934-35, 1935-36, 1936-37; McCaleb, Harding 1912-13, 1913-14, 1914-15, '15-16; McCarty, Arthur 1914-15; McClellan, Harvey 1937-38, 1938-39, 1940-41; McCray, Rodney 1979-80, 1980-81, 1981-82, 1982-83; McCray, Scooter 1978-79, 1980-81, 1981-82, 1982-83; McDevitt, Coleman 1929-30, 1930-31; McDonald, Bennie 1926-27, 1927-28; McIntyre, Jack 1945-46; McLendon, Jason 1990-91, 1991-92; McSwain, Mark 1983-84, 1984-85, 1985-86, 1986-87; Meiman, Joe 1971-72, 1972-73; Meiman, John 1975-76; Meyer, Bob 1937-38, 1938-39; Miles, Rick 1972-73; Miller, Lynn 1923-24, 1924-25, 1925-26; Miller, Clyde 1926-27, 1927-28; Minner, Gordon 1967-68; Minor, Greg 1991-92, 1992-93, 1993-94; Mitchell, Danny 1981-82, 1982-83, 1983-84, 1984-85; Monen, Si 1935-36, 1936-37, 1937-38; Moreman, Gerry 1953-54, 1954-55, 1955-56; Morgan, Jim 1954-55, 1955-56, 1956-57; Morgan, Sam 1915-16, 1917-18, 1918-19, 1919-20; Moriarty, John 1925-26, 1926-27; Morris, Landis 1917-18; Morton, Dwayne 1991-92, 1992-93, 1993-94; Muldoon, Phil 1941-42; Murphy, Allen 1972-73, 1973-74, 1974-75; Musterman, Ed 1930-31.

N Naber, Bob 1949-50, 1950-51, 1951-52; Neely, Greg 1968-69, 1969-70, 1970-71; Newkirk,

Richard 1918-19; Noble, Chuck 1951-52, 1952-53, 1953-54; ; O; Ogden, J.D. 1935-36; Ogilvie, Morgan 1943-44; Olliges, Will 1984-85, 1985-86, 1986-87, 1987-88; Olsen, Bud 1959-60, 1960-61, 1961-62; O'Neal, Lee 1944-45; Osborn, John 1944-45, 1945-46; Osborne, Jason 1993-94, 1994-95; Osborne, Paul 1921-22; Otte, H. F. 1943-44.

P Panther, Louis 1934-35, 1935-36, 1936-37, 1937-38; Panther, Dick 1935-36, 1936-37, 1937-38, 1938-39; Parker, Clyde 1944-45, 1945-46; Parry, J. F. 1943-44; Payne, Kenny 1985-86, 1986-87, 1987-88, 1988-89; Peloff, Dick 1960-61, 1961-62, 1962-63; Perkins, Bill 1968-69, 1969-70; Phillips, Bill 1941-42; Pike, Hall 1953-54, 1954-55; Potts, Ray 1947-48, 1948-49; Powell, Bill 1952-53, 1953-54; Price, Jim 1969-70, 1970-71, 1971-72; Protenic, Jim 1972-73, 1973-74; Prudhoe, John 1953-54, 1954-55; Pry, Paul 1969-70, 1970-71; Pulliam, Marty 1977-78, 1979-80, 1980-81, 1981-82.

R Ray, Jack 1959-60, 1960-61, 1961-62; Raymond, R. H. 1940-41; Rectenwald, William 1915-16; Redmon, L. H. 1919-20, 1920-21; Reeves, Kenny 1946-47, 1947-48, 1948-49, 1949-50; Reid, B. L. 1936-37, 1937-38; Reuther, Joe 1961-62, 1962-63, 1963-64; Reuther, John 1962-63, 1963-64, 1964-65; Ries, Bob 1944-45; Robinson, David 1985-86, 1986-87, 1987-88; Robison, Dick 1948-49, 1949-50, 1950-51, 1951-52; Rodgers, Clarence 1912-13, 1913-14, 1914-15; Rogers, Tick 1992-93, 1993-94, 1994-95; Rollins, Phil 1952-53, 1953-54, 1954-55, 1955-56; Roney, J. H. 1937-38, 1938-39; Rooks, Ron 1961-62, 1962-63, 1963-64; Rosenfield, Jimmy 1938-39; Rothman, Judd 1962-63, 1963-64, 1964-65; Rozier, Clifford 1992-93, 1993-94; Rubenstein, Ron 1958-59, 1959-60, 1960-61; Rubin, Roy 1950-51; Russak, Al 1952-53.

S Sanders, Charles 1934-35, 1935-36; Sawyer, Fred 1958-59, 1959-60, 1960-61; Schiengold, Pat 1921-22; Schreiber, Benny 1984-85, 1985-86, 1986-87; Search, Ted 1950-51; Selvy, Marv 1967-68, 1968-69; Shackelford, Roscoe 1954-55, 1955-56, 1956-57; Sheeley, Joe 1937-38, 1939-40, 1940-41; Silverstein, Phillip 1921-22; Simons, Matt 1993-94, 1994-95; Sims, Alvin 1993-94, 1994-95; Sipe, Kenny 1938-39, 1939-40, 1940-41, 1941-42; Slater, Walt 1937-38, 1938-39, 1939-40, 1940-41; Sloan, Wallace 1943-44; Smith, Beau Zach 1993-94, 1994-95; Smith, Dave 1975-76, 1976-77, 1977-78; Smith, Derek 1978-79, 1979-80, 1980-81, 1981-82; Smith, LaBradford 1987-88,1988,88-89, 1989-90, 1990-91; Smith, Sam 1963-64; Smith, Troy 1989-90, 1990-91, 1991-92, 1992-93; Snyder, Alva 1924-25; Sosnin, Hershell 1932-33; South, Regan 1933-34, 1934-35, 1935-36, 1936-37; Spencer, Charlie 1925-26, 1927-28, 1928-29, 1929-30; Spencer, Felton 1986-87, 1987-88, 1988-89, 1989-90; Stacey, Howard 1957-58, 1958-59, 1959-60; Stallings, Ron 1970-71, 1971-72; Stevens, Shelby 1915-16; Stone, Kip 1990-91, 1991-92; Stone, Reid 1941-42; Strickler, Frank 1913-14; Stripling, Jon 1962-63; Strull, Asher 1931-32, 1932-33, 1933-34, 1934-35; Struve, Dudley 1915-16; Studer, John 1968-69, 1969-70, 1970-71; Stultz, Elwood 1939-40, 1940-41; Stultz, John 1935-36, 1936-37; Sullivan, Bill 1950-51, 1951-52, 1952-53; Sullivan, Everick 1988-89, 1989-90, 1990-91, 1991-92; Summers, Harold 1938-39, 1939-40; Sumpter, Barry 1983-84, 1984-85.

T Taylor, A. P. 1941-42; Terry, Prentiss 1915-16; Thomas, Ron 1970-71, 1971-72; Thompson, Billy 1982-83, 1983-84, 1984-85, 1985-86; Thompson, Williard "Tommy" 1929-30, 1930-31, 1931-32;

Threlkeld, Billy 1931-32, 1932-33, 1933-34, 1934-35; Tieman, Roger 1957-58, 1958-59, 1959-60; Todd, Grover 1913-14; Trenholme, William 1944-45; Turner, John 1958-59, 1959-60, 1960-61; Turner, Bobby 1976-77, 1977-78, 1978-79; Tyra, Charlie 1954-55, 1955-56, 1956-57.

U Unseld, Wes 1965-66, 1966-67, 1967-68.

V Valentine, Robbie 1982-83, 1983-84, 1984-85, 1985-86; Vance, Bruce 1919-20; Van Wagner, Wiley 1931-32; Varoscak, John 1957-58; Vilcheck, Al 1969-70, 1970-71, 1971-72; Vonderbrueggen, Lucian 1943-44.

W Waggener, Gil 1946-47, 1947-48, 1948-49; Wagner, A. T. 1938-39; Wagner, Milt 1981-82, 1982-83, 1983-84, 1985-86; Walker, Paul 1947-48; Walker, Samaki 1994-95; Walsh, Knobby 1945-46, 1946-47; Watkins, Jerry 1960-61; Wayne, Jeff 1973-74; Webb, Derwin 1989-90, 1990-91, 1991-92, 1992-93; Weber, Eddie 1924-25, 1925-26, 1926-27, 1927-28; Weber, Robert 1938-39, 1939-40;

Wedekind, J. B. 1934-35; West, Chris 1982-83, 1984-85, 1985-86, 1986-87; Wellman, Bob 1950-51; Wheat, DeJuan 1993-94, 1994-95; White, Andy 1961-62, 1962-63; White, Chris 1985-86, 1986-87; Whitehead, Eddie 1964-65, 1965-66; Whitehouse, Harold 1943-44; Whitfield, Ike 1973-74, 1974-75; Wilkie, Ray 1944-45; Williams, Harlan 1947-48; Williams, Keith 1986-87, 1987-88, 1988-89, 1989-90; Williams, Larry 1975-76, 1976-77, 1977-78, 1978-79; Willig, Armin 1930-31, 1931-32, 1932-33, 1933-34; Willingter, Paul 1936-37; Wilson, Rick 1974-75, 1975-76, 1976-77, 1977-78; Wine, Robbie 1992-93, 1993-94, 1994-95; Wingfield, Tremaine 1990-91, 1991-92; Witt, Jeff 1984-85, 1985-86, 1986-87, 1987-88; Woods, Chris 1974-75; Wright, Les 1930-31, 1931-32, 1932-33, 1933-34; Wright, Poncho 1979-80, 1980-81, 1981-82.

Y Yeager, Arthur 1921-22.

Z Zeller, Rod 1943-44; Zirkle, Charles 1936-37

TRIVIA ANSWERS

1. Georgetown College

2. Charlie Tyra

3. U of L defeated Morehead State, 72-59, at the 1984 NCAA Mideast Regional in Milwaukee.

4. Wes Unseld, who scored 45 points against Georgetown College in 1967.

5. Charlie Tyra (vs. Notre Dame in 18956) and Butch Beard (vs. Bradley in 1967).

6. Jeff Hall

7. Nineteen, starting with a 50-27 loss to Georgetown College in the next-to-last game during the 1938-39 season and continuing through the first 17 games of the next season.

8. Keith LeGree

9. Kentucky

10. Western Kentucky

11. DeJuan Wheat

12. Illinois and Northwestern

13. Iowa and Michigan are both 0-2; Wisconsin is 0-1

14. Mississippi

15. Massachusetts — March 2, 1996

16. 61,612 watched the Cardinals lose to Georgetown during a 1992 national semifinal game at the Superdome in New Orleans

17. The Boston Celtics and the Minneapolis Lakers

18. The Cards defeated Notre Dame, 85-75, on December 22, 1956. However, Freedom Hall did not become U of L's home until the following season.

19. Pervis Ellison in 1986

20. Don Goldstein in 1959

21. Edwin Kornfield

22. Felton Spencer, 62.8 percent

23. On March 22, 1958 UK (third in the UKIT) and

Seattle (third in the Bluegrass) played for the national championship in Freedom Hall.

24. Cliff Rozier, 1994

25. Jack Coleman, who topped the 1,000 mark in 1949

26. DeJuan Wheat

27. True

28. Wes Unseld and Butch Beard

29. Georgetown College and Kentucky Wesleyan

30. Western Kentucky holds a 37-31 advantage in the series, despite the fact that the Hilltoppers have won only once since 1961.

31. UCLA

32. Kansas State

33. Jack Coleman (1948-50), Charlie Tyra (1955-57), John Turner (1959-61), John Reuther (1963-65), Allen Murphy (1973-75), and Darrell Griffith (1978-80)

34. DePaul

35. Junior Bridgeman

36. Darrell Griffith

37. True

38. On November 30, 1953, the Cardinals defeated Kentucky Wesleyan, 112-69, in the first game of the season.

COLLEGE SPORTS HANDBOOKS

Stories, Stats & Stuff About America's Favorite Teams

U. of Arizona	Basketball	Arizona Wildcats Handbook
U. of Arkansas	Basketball	Razorbacks Handbook
Baylor	Football	Bears Handbook
Clemson	Football	Clemson Handbook
U. of Colorado	Football	Buffaloes Handbook
U. of Florida	Football	Gator Tales
Georgia Tech	Basketball	Yellow Jackets Handbook
Indiana U.	Basketball	Hoosier Handbook
Iowa State	Sports	Cyclones Handbook
U. of Kansas	Basketball	Crimson & Blue Handbook
Kansas State	Sports	Kansas St Wildcat Handbook
LSU	Football	Fighting Tigers Handbook
U. of Miami	Football	Hurricane Handbook
U. of Michigan	Football	Wolverines Handbook
U. of Missouri	Basketball	Tiger Handbook
U. of Nebraska	Football	Husker Handbook
U. of N. Carolina	Basketball	Tar Heels Handbook
N.C. State	Basketball	Wolfpack Handbook
U. of Oklahoma	Football	Sooners Handbook
Penn State	Football	Nittany Lions Handbook
U. of S. Carolina	Football	Gamecocks Handbook
Stanford	Football	Stanford Handbook
Syracuse	Sports	Orange Handbook
U. of Tennessee	Football	Volunteers Handbook
U. of Texas	Football	Longhorns Handbook
Texas A&M	Football	Aggies Handbook
Texas Tech	Sports	Red Raiders Handbook
Virginia Tech	Football	Hokies Handbook
Wichita State	Sports	Shockers Handbook
U. of Wisconsin	Football	Badgers Handbook

Also:

Big 12 Handbook: Stories, Stats and Stuff About The Nation's Best
    Football Conference
The Top Fuel Handbook: Stories, Stats and Stuff About Drag Racing's
    Most Powerful Class

For ordering information call Midwest Sports Publications at:

1-800-492-4043